ACCOUNT

A Simple Guide to Financial and
Managerial Accounting for
Beginners

By Kevin Ellis

professional before attempting any techniques outlined in this book.

By reading this document, the reader agrees that under no circumstances is the author responsible for any losses, direct or indirect, which are incurred as a result of the use of information contained within this document, including, but not limited to, — errors, omissions, or inaccuracies.

Table of Contents

INTRODUCTION

Thank you for purchasing, "Accounting: A Simple Guide to Financial and Managerial Accounting for Beginners." I hope you find this book informative and useful.

If you are looking for a guide that will help you gain a good understanding of accounting, this is the perfect book for you. It is designed to provide the reader with a basic but adequate understanding of financial and managerial accounting. You have to realize that accounting is a vast subject, and you cannot become an expert just by reading a single book. However, this book will provide you with enough information on accounting to help you understand everything you need as a beginner.

When you think of accounting, the first thing that comes to mind is crunching numbers. But an accountant does a lot more than that. Very few people recognize all that goes into accounting until they have involved in it themselves. This book will help you get familiar with all of this and more.

I am sure you are thinking, why is accounting important? Well, accounting involves a comprehensive and systematic record keeping of financial transactions related to any business. Accounting is important for various reasons. It is not just about keeping books or filing taxes. Even though these are two of the main tasks involved in it, there are many other facets involved in accounting too. In business, accounting will involve setting up accounting systems and preparing reports or statements related to all finances. There is a lot more than these things as well that you will soon learn. The point is, accounting is considered the language of business. It will help you understand how a business works and where it is thriving or declining. It allows you to ascertain what the financial position is for a business. Accounting reports allow management to determine what the business position is and what steps they need to take to improve the current position. Accounting is required for all business transactions. It will help to record, classify, and summarize of all the transactions. This enables proper analysis and creation of balance sheets, trial balance, and other financial documents.

Accounting plays an important role in decision making, controlling processes, and planning. The documents that are factored in all of this are created with the help of accounting. The methodical documenting involved in accounting will also prevent or reduce any incidence of theft or fraud in the business. Proper accounting will allow any business to run efficiently. It will enable effectiveness and accuracy in all activities. This will lead to better productivity and enable the management to make better decisions regarding the business.

In business, accounting will be involved in various functions. It is required for planning a budget. A proper budget will help the business run systematically. It will help to make strategies, save money, and also to prevent expenditure beyond what is specified in a budget. Records of financial statements in the business are required for a budget to be created. These documents will be available through accounting.

When you need a loan from a bank or any lender, you will be required to show your financial statements. These documents are only available if your business has a proper accounting system. This is how you can present any financial books to the bank. It will include records of profits, assets, or liabilities. Loans are only given out after scrutiny of such financial records.

Accounting takes care of the basic but crucial function of keeping records for a business. A business needs records to allow smooth running. Records have to be collected and organized well. They also have to be interpreted so the end-user can understand and make viable decisions based on these records.

The statements obtained through accounting will influence decision-making and provide information to investors in the business. Executives of a business cannot make sound decisions when they don't have access to accurate financial statements. If they don't have these documents, they will fail to achieve the objectives of their business. The lack of financial records will also have a negative impression on any investors in the business. Accounts will help them keep track of the progress or decline of any organization.

You can see that accounting is important in many different ways, and probably more than you previously expected.

Since this book is specifically aimed at providing information on financial and managerial accounting, let us get a basic introduction to them as well.

What is financial accounting? Financial accounting involves summarizing, analyzing, and reporting financial transactions that are related to a particular business. It is focused on providing useful information for the benefit of external users.

What is managerial accounting? Managerial accounting is concerned with accounting information that managers can use to help them in making better decisions so they can improve their management of the company's operations. It is focused on internal decision making, unlike financial accounting.

The book will cover a lot of topics, including:

- The accounting equation
- GAAP and IFRS

ACCOUNTING

- Financial accounting
- Managerial accounting
- Financial statements
- Recording statements

All of these topics will be covered in detail to help you understand better. So, if you are ready, let us get started without further ado!

Chapter One: Introduction to the Accounting Equation

If you want to be an expert in the field of accounting, you have to familiarize yourself with the accounting equation. The double-entry accounting system uses the accounting equation as its basis. A company's balance sheet will display the accounting equation such that the sum of shareholders equity and the company's liabilities will be equal to the total assets of the company. It will ensure that the balance sheet of a company remains balanced based on this double-entry system. Every entry that is made on the debit side will have a corresponding entry made on the credit side.

The accounting equation formula is as follows for sole proprietorship:

Total Assets=Liabilities + Owner's Equity.

For a corporation, the formula will be:

Total assets=Liabilities + Stockholder's equity.

Calculation of the equation

- The accounting equation forms the basis of the balance sheet.
- The total number of assets if a company has to be located on the balance sheet for a period.
- All the liabilities have to be calculated and totaled under a separate listing on the same balance sheet.
- The total shareholder's equity has to be located and totaled. This has to be added to the total of the liabilities.
- The total assets will have to equal the sum of the liabilities and equity.
- The points to remember are:
- The accounting equation is the foundation of the double-entry system.
- The balance sheet of a company will show that the total assets of a company are equal to the sum of its liabilities and shareholder's equity.
- The assets are any of the valuable resources that the company owns.
- The liabilities are any obligations held by the company.
- The shareholder's equity and liabilities will represent how the company's assets are financed.

- It will be a liability if financing is done through debt. If financing is down by issuing equity shares, it will be displayed as shareholders equity.

What is an Asset?

Any resources or a property possessed by an entity that not only has a certain monetary value but will also provide some form of economic benefit is referred to as an asset. An asset not only provides some benefit to a business but also helps improve its value. So, anything that a business owns is referred to as an asset. Assets are classified according to their liquidity, their use by a business, or the physical existence. Assets will include any cash or cash equivalents and liquid assets. This may consist of treasury bills or certificates of deposits. The amount of money that is owed by the customers to the company for product sales or services is known as account receivables. Assets will also include inventory.

Anything that the company owns will be considered an asset. This includes land, buildings, inventory, receivable accounts, cash, investments, and equipment.

Examples of assets include:

- Buildings
- Prepaid insurance
- Petty cash

ACCOUNTING

- Cash
- Inventory
- Land improvements
- Equipment
- Goodwill
- Temporary investments
- Accounts receivable
- Asset Accounts will usually have debit balances.

Asset accounts with credit balances are Contra assets. Such contra asset accounts include:

- Accumulated depletion
- Accumulated depreciation buildings
- Accumulated depreciation equipment
- Allowance for doubtful accounts

In balance sheets, assets will be classified in a certain way. This means that the assets will be put under distinct categories or groupings. Accounts use this classification to bring more order to the balance sheet.

Assets will be classified in the following way on a balance sheet:

- Current assets
- Investments
- Property, plant, and equipment
- Intangible assets
- Other assets

Classification of assets

Assets can be classified according to their liquidity. Liquidity refers to the ability of an asset being converted into cash. Based on the liquidity, assets are classified into current assets or fixed assets. Any asset which can be readily converted into cash like inventory, short-term investments, stock, bank balances, bills receivable, or prepaid expenses will be classified as current assets. Any short-term asset will be referred to as a current asset. These assets are also referred to as liquid assets. Any asset, which cannot be readily converted into cash and this of a fixed nature, are referred to as fixed assets. Before these assets can be converted into cash, they usually have an extensive procedure for their sale. Examples of fixed assets include machinery and equipment, land and building, furniture and fixtures, and so on. Fixed assets are also known as long-term assets, hard assets, or even current assets. Fixed assets are subject to depreciation, whereas current assets aren't. Depreciation refers to the decrease in the value of an asset.

Assets can also be classified according to their physical existence. The two classifications of assets, according to their physical existence, are tangible assets and intangible assets. Any assets, which you can touch, feel, and see are referred to as tangible assets. All fixed assets are tangible assets. Also, there are certain current assets like cash or inventory, which can be considered to be as tangible assets. Any asset, which you cannot physically touch, see, or feel are known as intangible assets. The goodwill of a company, brand value, or trademark is intangible assets. Even if they don't have a physical existence, these assets influence the value of a business.

An asset can also be classified based on its use by the business. According to this classification, there are two types of assets, and they are operating assets or non-operating assets. Any asset that is used for day-to-day operations in business is referred to as an operating asset. All the assets that business users to produce the products or services it offers are referred to as operating assets. Examples of operating assets include bank balance, cash balance, inventory, plant apartment, and so on. Any assets that don't fall under the previous category are referred to as a non-operating asset. A business also has certain assets, which it doesn't use with day-to-day operations. These assets are, however, important for meeting its current and future needs. Examples of non-operating assets include any real estate property or excess cash reserves that are reduced for operational purposes.

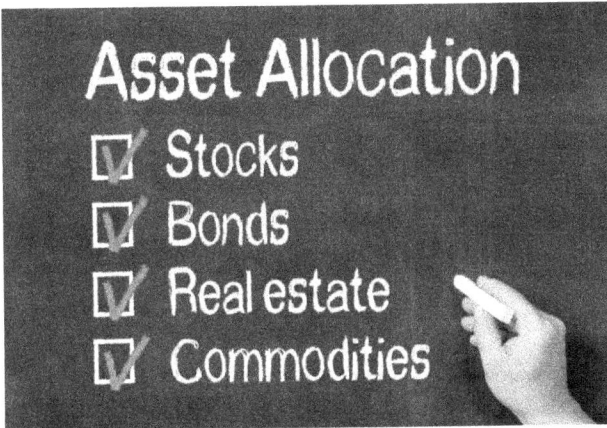

What is a Liability?

Liabilities comprise of what the company will usually owe others or have to pay so they can continue running. These are the obligations of the company. Liabilities include debt, rent, utilities, wages, taxes, salaries, loans, etc.

A liability can be viewed in two ways:

- It is viewed as claims by creditors against the assets of the company
- It is viewed as a source of the assets of the company.

Liabilities will also include any advance money that is received for further services. This amount revives will be received as asset cash but has not been earned yet. This is why the company will defer to revenue reporting and report it as a liability instead. It will be marked under customer deposits or unearned revenue.

The following are examples of liability accounts in the balance sheet of a company:

- Accounts payable
- Interest payable
- Notes payable
- Wages payable
- Income taxes payable
- Customer deposits
- Salaries payable
- Other accrued expenses payable
- Lawsuits payable
- Unearned revenue
- Bonds payable
- Warranty liability

These liability accounts will have credit balances.

A liability account with a debit balance is a contra liability. If there is a debit balance in a liability account, it is contrary to the usual credit balance of the liability account.

Contra liability account examples include:

- Debt issue costs
- Bond issue costs

- Discount on notes payable
- Discount on bonds payable
- Liabilities classification

On the balance sheet, liability accounts and contra liability accounts will usually be classified. They will be put into distinct categories or classifications in the following order:

- Current liabilities
- Long term liabilities
- Commitments

The commitments of the company may be legally binding, but they will not be considered as a liability until some goods or services are received. Such commitments may include signing contracts for future services. If a commitment is of a significant amount, it has to be disclosed in the notes on the balance sheet.

Form vs. substance

When a certain asset is leased, it may appear like rental of it on the surface. However, in substance, it can be part of a binding agreement for purchasing the asset and financing it through monthly payouts. It is important for accounts to look past the visible form and to focus on the actual substance of a transaction. In substance, if a lease is an agreement for purchasing an asset and creating a note payable, the asset and liability have to be reported in the balance sheet and accounts.

Contingent liabilities

The following are three contingent liabilities examples:

- The warranty for the products of a company
- Guarantee of the loan of another party
- Lawsuits that are filed against the company

Such contingent liabilities will be potential liabilities because they will be dependent on future events that may or may not occur, and therefore, they may or may not turn into an actual liability.

For instance, take the case of a company being sued by a former employee for $200000 in wrongful termination. In this case, do you think the $200000 is a liability for the company? This would depend on two things. It is not a liability if the company has proper reasons and was justified in the termination of the employee. In such a case, the lawsuit will be frivolous. However, if the company had actually acted improperly and the employee was wrongfully terminated, there will be an income statement loss and thus a balance sheet liability.

Accounting rules for such liabilities exist. According to these rules, in case of a probable contingent loss and if the loss amount can be estimated, liability has to be recorded in the balance sheet with a loss being recorded in the income statement. In case of a remote contingent loss, liability or loss does not have to be recorded. It will not have to be included in the financial statements. In case the contingent loss is somewhere between these two conditions, it should be disclosed as a note in the financial statement.

Current vs. Long term liabilities

In case a company has a loan payable that has monthly payments due for several years, the principal amount that is due in the next twelve months has to be reported as a current liability in the balance sheet. The rest has to be reported under long-term liabilities. The interest of the loan pertaining to the future does not have to be recorded, the unpaid interest until the date of that balance sheet is the only liability recorded.

Notes to financial statements

You may have noticed how we mentioned notes repeatedly above. The notes to the financial statement can be very revealing and provide important information. These notes should be given special attention while going through the balance sheet of a company.

What is a Stockholders' Equity?

The total assets of a company minus its total liabilities are what will comprise of stockholder's equity. It represents the money that would be returned to all the stockholders in case the company assets were liquidated after debts were paid off. Stockholders equity includes retained earnings, and these are equal to the net earning percentage that the shareholders did not receive as dividends. These retained earnings are like savings because they arena total cumulative profit kept aside for future use.

The stockholder's equity will report how much was invested by owners into the company as well as the net income of the company that was withdrawn or distributed.

If you rearrange the accounting equation, you will get the following:

Owner's equity=Assets-Liabilities

Owner's equity will be marked on the balance sheet of a sole proprietorship company. In the case of a corporation, it will be marked as stockholder's equity.

Stockholders equity accounts will include:

- Common stock
- Preferred stock
- Retained earnings
- Accumulated other comprehensive income
- Paid-in capital in excess of par value
- Paid in capital from treasury stock and so on.

Owner's equity, as well as stockholder's equity, will have credit balances.

A contra owner's equity account is an owner's equity account, which has a debit balance. A debit balance is contrary to an owner's equity account because it usually has a credit balance.

In a corporatism balance sheet, the stockholder's equity section is:

- Treasury stock
- Retained earnings
- Paid in capital
- Accumulated other comprehensive income

Owner's equity vs. the company's market value

Asset amounts will report the cost of assets when the transaction takes place. This means that they won't reflect current market values that are fair. Since the fair market value of these assets is not reported, the owner's equity will not indicate the fair market value of that company.

Owner's equity and Temporary accounts

Income statement accounts include revenues, expenses, gains, and losses. Revenue and gain will cause an increase in owner's equity. The owner's equity will decrease expenses and losses. Assets will increase when a company performs a device so the owner's equity will also increase at the end of that accounting year when the device revenues account is being closed.

Accounting Must Balance

Accurate record keeping in the company will ensure that there is always a balance in the accounting equation. This means that the left side will always equal the right side. The accounting balance will be maintained because at least two accounts will be affected by a single transaction. For instance, take a scenario where a company takes a loan from a bank. In this case, the assets of the company increase, and so will the liabilities. It will be in the same amount on both sides. When inventory is purchased with cash, there will be an increase in one asset while another will decrease. The accounting system is called the double entry system because every transaction affects two or more accounts. All these transactions are tracked by keeping records in the general ledger of the company. Every account in this ledger will be designated accordingly - asset, revenue, liability, owner's equity, gain, loss, or expense.

Assets -
Liabilities =
Equity

Chapter Two: Understanding GAAP

What is GAAP?

The full form of GAAP is Generally Accepted Accounting Principles. A common compilation of agreed accounting principles, methods, and standards that industry and their employees must obey while submitting the financial statements are referred to as generally accepted accounting principles.

Many companies mainly use GAAP for the following purposes:

- Organize all the financial information to accounting records.
- Collecting the accounting records and making a financial statement.
- Providing few supporting documents.

GAAP usually requires the company to maintain a minimum level of consistency in their financial statements, mainly for the investors to make their work of analyzing and getting useful information about the company easier and faster. GAAP also helps to compare the financial statements of different companies.

The following are the main aim of GAAP:

ACCOUNTING

1. Principle of regularity

As GAAP rules and regulations are set as a standard, the accountant has to stick to it.

2. Principle of consistency

Accountants have to be consistent and apply the same rules and regulations in the entire process to avoid mistakes and discrepancies. The accountants have to mention and explain everything, and even if there's a minute change, they have to reason it out.

3. Principle of sincerity

The accountant tries her/his best to represent an exact condition of a company's financial condition.

4. Principle of the permanence of methods

The methods and techniques used in financial reporting have to be followed consistently.

5. Principle of non-compensation

Not only the positives but also the negatives have to be mentioned with clear details and without any expectations of debt compensation.

6. Principle of prudence

Focusing mainly on financial data representation with clear facts.

7. Principle of continuity

It should be assumed that the company is still running while calculating financial values.

8. Principle of periodicity

Everything entered should be classified into their relevant timelines.

9. Principle of materiality

The accountants should mention every minute detail in financial reports.

10. Principle of utmost good faith

It says everyone involved must maintain transactions genuinely.

GAAP includes the following:

- Financial statement presentation
- Properties
- Liabilities
- Equity
- Revenue
- Expenditures
- Business combination
- Derivatives and hedging
- Fair value
- Foreign currency
- Leases
- Nonmonetary transactions

- Subsequent events
- Industry-specific accounting like airlines, healthcare, and other activities.

These industries specified accounting in GAAP might be different in transactions than the others.

GAAP vs. IFRS

GAAP is mainly followed in the United States of American companies and is set by the financial accounting standards board (FASB). In other parts of the world, instead of GAAP, International Financial Reporting Standards (IFRS) are used and are issued by the international accounting standards board (IASB).

Since 2002, both the IASB and FASB have been working hard to merge GAAP and IFRS. As a result of this hard work, in 2007, the SEC had removed the requirement of a non-US company in the USA to comply with their financial statements with GAAP if it is already reconciled with IFRS. Before this, a non-US company in the USA had to comply with their financial documents with GAAP for trading in US transactions.

So, following are the differences between GAAP and IFRS accounting:

Locally vs. Globally

As mentioned, IFRS accounting is used in more than 110 countries and is globally accepted whereas GAAP is used only in America and has its own rules and regulations making it more difficult for American companies to do business outside.

Rules vs. Principles

One of the main differences between GAAP and IFRS accounting is the technique used in the accounting process. GAAP is strictly based on rules, and IFRS is more about overall patterns and is based on principle. As GAAP sticks on rules, everything is mostly clear so interpretation and exceptions are uncommon whereas in IFRS, even though accounts are the same, as it's based on principle, there can be different interpretations.

Inventory methods

In the GAAP method, they permit the Last In, First Out (LIFO) method for inventory estimates, whereas, in IFRS, a LIFO method is not allowed. LIFO method cannot be reliable as it's not accurate with inventory flow.

Inventory reversal

Not only do they have different tracking inventory methods. GAAP and IFRS accounting have a different policy in inventory write-down reversal. Whenever there's an increase on the market value of an asset, GAAP doesn't allow in reversing the inventory write-down, which reflects that GAAP is very careful with inventory reversal and doesn't implicate the changes on the market, whereas in IFRS the company can reverse the inventory write-down.

Developmental costs

The developmental cost of a company can be counted as an investment as long as they meet certain requirements on the company in IFRS. But in GAAP, the developmental cost would be considered as expenditure the same year and not as an investment.

Intangible assets

Research and development or advertising costs come under intangible assets. So, in IFRS, since they are principle-based accounting, they are very considerate about intangible assets and see if the assets can be beneficial in the future to the company. But GAAP considers intangible assets to be fair market value and nothing beyond.

Income statements

In GAAP, unusual or extraordinary items are segregated and mentioned below the net income portion of the income statement whereas in IFRS; these are not separated and included in the income statement.

Classification of liabilities

In GAAP, the debts of the company are separated into two sections. One is the current liability in which the company will be able to pay a certain amount at a certain period of time, and the other is the noncurrent liability where the company cannot pay the amount in that period of time. In IFRS, they don't have any differentiation, and all debts are put in one balance sheet.

Fixed assets

Fixed assets are the properties, furniture, and equipment of a company. So, in GAAP accounting, they value the assets using the cost of the model when bought minus the damage, repairing, and maintenance is done till date. Whereas in IFRS, they consider the cost of the asset by checking the cost in current time minus the damage, repairing, and maintenance done till date and is called the revaluation model.

Quality characteristics

Out of all, this is one of the main differences between GAAP and IFRS. GAAP functions on the hierarchy of characteristics like relevance, reliability, comparability, and understandability, to make the correct decision based on user-specific circumstances. IFRS also works similarly just for the fact that it doesn't decide based on user-specific circumstances of an individual.

Compliance

In accounting, a company's financial accounts and reports should be managed according to the federal laws and regulations, and it is called Compliance.

A company is bound to share every single minute detail to its shareholders and the regulatory authorities such as the Securities and Exchange Commission (SEC). It's very important for the procedures to be done correctly for recording, verifying, and reporting the total asset value of a company, liabilities, debts, and expenses.

In 2002, the Sarbanes-Oxley Act was applied as several scandals in corporate accounting were found. The act set a new standard s in accounting and internal auditing of these companies. The Sarbanes-Oxley Act has 11 titles, which explain the accounting and financial reporting compliance requirements.

Title 1: Public Company Accounting Oversight Board (PCAOB)

PCAOB was then established as a public agency whose function was to regulate, set policies and discipline accounting firms that used to provide auditing services for public traded companies.

Title 2: Auditor Independence

Before Sarbanes-Oxley came into action. All the auditing companies that were monitoring the accounting work of public companies were regulating on its own. Not only that, but also these companies were also consulting for the companies they were supposed to audit for. So, to avoid all these, this title was established to standardize the external auditor independence, which included auditor approval requirements, partner rotation, and reporting requirements.

Title 3: Corporate Responsibility

The above title specifically mentioned that the senior executives in the company were solely responsible for completing and submitting the financial reports of the company without any errors or mistakes. For example, the responsibility of certifying and approving the financial report contents was given to the corporations' senior-most officers like the CEO and the CFO.

Title 4: Enhanced Financial Disclosure

This title established some additional requirements for the transaction of the company's finance in various fields such as the stock transactions of corporate officers or off-balance sheet transactions. For compliance assurance of financial reports and disclosure, internal controls were also employed.

Title 5: Analyst Conflicts of Interest

Most of the primary investors of company's share had lost their trust in security analysts, so in order to restore their lost trust, this title was established in which the security analysts had to follow the code of conduct where they had to disclose any minute details of even small conflicts.

Title 6: Commission Resources and Authority

This title, like the previous one, was meant to show the security professionals work clearly for the restoration of investor's trust and confidence. It also allows the SEC's authority to either warn or exempt analysts from practicing.

Title 7: Studies and Reports

This title was beneficial as the Comptroller General and the SEC were asked to research and submit the report of their studies. The research included the impact of credit rating agencies on the securities market, the effects of consolidating the accounting firms, and involvement of investment banks in the accounting scandals of Enron, Global Crossing, and others.

Title 8: Corporate and Criminal Fraud Accountability

This title had set specific penalties for those who try to fraud the compliance investigations, and the 'whistleblowers' were also given protection. This title is also called the Corporate and Criminal Fraud Act of 2002.

Title 9: White Collar Crime Penalty Enhancement

This title stated that the penalties for white-collar crimes and conspiracies would be more severe. This title stated that the corporate officers would be facing severe criminal charges if they fail to submit and get their financial reports certified. This title is also called as the White-Collar Crime Penalty Enhancement Act of 2002.

Title 10: Corporate Tax Returns

This title states that the CEO is solely responsible for the signing of the company's tax return.

Title 11: Corporate Fraud Accountability

This title is also known as the Corporate Fraud Accountability Act of 2002. This title enforced the fraud in corporate organizations and tampering of the company's record to criminal charges. Not only did they revise the sentencing guidelines, but also gave the SEC full right to stop doubtful transactions (huge or very unusual) till they were fully investigated.

Due to these strict rules and regulations, many companies find it difficult to cope with. Though many of the companies have proved themselves to be eligible and honest, the tight rules and requirements have shown the company's weakness and incompetence in the accounting systems. So, some of the companies have improved the accounting and internal processes, while the other has hired outside accounting firms to handle the accounting compliance.

Types of Accounting

There are three types of accounting and they are financial accounting, cost accounting, and managerial accounting.

Financial accounting

Financial accounting is mainly concerned with the record keeping which is directed towards the preparation of financial statements like the income statement and balance sheet. There are three main purposes that financial accounting serves. The first is that it helps to record transactions which are not just related to the business but also affect it. Financial accounting also helps in the preparation of necessary accounts and financial statements as the wand by the statutes and concerned loss. It also helps the owners of a business understand whether the businesses growing or not over a period. Financial accounting is the accounting for expenses, revenues, assets, and the liabilities. This is often restricted to all the published financial reports and is in direct contrast to internal branches of accounting like cost accounting.

Cost accounting

As the name suggests, this is the process of accounting for cost. It's a systematic procedure to determine the unit cost of an output produced or any service rendered by business. The primary function of cost accounting is to a certain the cost of a product and to help the management control its cost. Cost accounting deals with the classification, allocation, recording, summarization, and the reporting of current as well as prospective cost. Financial accounting as well as cost accounting are associated with the accumulation and the presentation of information for serving the needs of a management as well as other interested parties.

Management accounting

Management of any organization is primarily concerned with the supply of information, which is useful for the management in decision-making and for the efficient running of the business. The main idea of Management accounting is profit maximization. Management accounting is the reproduction of the final accounts or statements in such a manner that it helps the management to make decisions and to control activities. Management accounting is the term which is used to describe the accounting systems, methods, and techniques which, coupled with special knowledge and ability, assess the management in its task of minimizing losses in maximizing the profits. Management accounting is essentially a combination of financial accounting along with cost accounting.

You will learn in detail about all these types of accounting in the subsequent chapters.

Chapter Three: Financial Accounting

Financial accounting is one of the specialized branches of accounting. It is used for keeping track of the financial transactions of a company. There are standardized guidelines that are used for recording, summarizing, and presenting the transactions in a financial report or statement. This can be in the form of something like a balance sheet or an income statement. Such financial statements are issued by companies quite routinely under a schedule. These financial statements are considered external because of the fact that they can be accessed by people outside of that company. This includes owners, stockholders, or moneylenders. This information will be accessible to even more people if the stock of that company is publicly traded. In that case, the financial statements are likely to circulate around more and will reach the hands of customers, employees, competitors, analysts, etc. You have to know that the main purpose of financial accounting is not reporting a company's value. In fact, it is actually so that others have just enough information that will allow them to assess the company's value for themselves. Different people can use external financial statements in different ways. The common rules of financial accounting are called accounting standards or known as generally accepted accounting principles. You will learn more about this later in the book. The Financial Accounting Standards Board in the U.S. is responsible for developing the standards and principles for accounting. If the stock of a company is traded publicly, the company is compelled to comply with the SEC's reporting requirements. The book will cover all of this in more detail.

Accounting Principles

In the field of accounting, there are some basic rules and guidelines that govern it, and these general rules are known as basic accounting principles and guidelines. Some of the detailed complicated, and legalistic accounting rules and guidelines are completely based on these accounting principles. The basic accounting principles and guidelines are also used by the financial accounting standards board (FASB) to set their own detailed and comprehensive set of accounting rules and standards.

Generally accepted accounting principles (GAAP) is comprised of three important rules, and they are:

- The basic accounting principles and guidelines.
- Rules and standards that are set by the financial accounting standard board and accounting principle board (apt).
- Commonly accepted industry practices.

When a company is making its financial statements public, while preparing those financial statements, the company is supposed to follow the generally accepted accounting principles. Also, when a company's stock trading is done publicly, the federal law has to audit the company's financial statements using independent public accountants. It has to be proven by both the companies' accountants and the independent public accounts that the company's financial statements and the related notes on the statement were made following the generally accepted accounting principles (GAAP).

It is proven that generally accepted accounting principles are very beneficial as it standardizes and regulates accounting definition, assumptions, and procedures. We can make sure that a company's method of preparing its financial statement is consistent throughout the year using generally accepted accounting principles. Even though there might be some exceptions, it can be said assuredly while differentiating companies or the company's financial statistics to the statistics of the industry. Since the financial transactions have become very complex, accordingly generally accepted accounting principles have become complex.

Functions of Accounting

Every business engages in several transactions. It can become quite difficult to keep track of all these transactions, and this is where accounting steps in. Accounting helps to keep the systematic record of all the financial transactions conducted by the business. By maintaining letters and financial statements, it becomes easier to stay on top of the financial transactions. Accounting also helps to secure properties owned by the business. A business can reach insolvency if there is an unauthorized dissipation of assets. Accounting helps to create a system that protects the assets of a business from unwarranted or unjustified use. Accounting involves not only the keeping of records but also the maintaining of financial statements. Financial statements communicate important results about businesses operating capacity to interested parties like creditors, government officials, proprietors, investors, or even employees. Apart from this, and the accounting system also enables that a business meets all the legal requirements put on by the federal and the State governments. The various statements that a business needs to file like sales tax returns and income tax returns.

Advantages of Accounting

There are various advantages of accounting and have been mentioned in this section.

The books of accounts provide a detailed and systematic record of all the transactions of a business. It is not humanly possible for one person to remember all the transactions made by the business. So, accounting helps by keeping track of all the transactions related to the day-to-day operations of a business. Financial statements like profit and loss account, trading account, and the balance sheet help understand the performance of a business. Based on the concept of consistency, a business needs to follow the same rules of financial, maintaining its books of records. Since all the books of records are maintained according to the same principles, it makes it easier to compare them. So, you can compare the performance of the business by using its financial statements from the previous years and measuring it against the present year. It gives a bird's eye view of how well a business is doing. It also identifies the areas where the business is lacking.

The primary aim of any business is to on profits. So, most of the decisions made by the business owner of the management will be directed towards attaining this objective. Financial statements make it easier for the top management to make decisions about a business and its future. The systematic records help to ascertain whether certain aspects of the business are doing well or not. It also helps to determine the answer certain important questions like what the selling price of the goods must be or decisions regarding the procurement of the necessary raw materials.

Maintaining the books of accounts is also quite helpful in legal matters. A record of all business transactions can be provided as satisfactory evidence in a court of law. Apart from this, financial transactions provide necessary information to all the interested parties like the creditors, investors, business owners, governments, and so on. When this information is provided to the interest that groups, it becomes easier for them to make any decisions related to the business. For instance, if the financial position of the business is favorable, then it will be easier for a business to attain loans from its creditors. Every business needs to pay certain taxes. Taxes can't be paid if there is no record of proper financial transactions by keeping track of all the expenses are transactions; it becomes easier for a business to pay its dues. Fashion statements also provide information, which is necessary to plan certain operations like fear, cash requirement of the business, production, and so on. It also helps to make business forecast too. The financial health of a business can be gauged based on its financial statements. Apart from this, it also helps with the valuation of a business.

Now that you are aware of the different benefits accounting offers and the purpose it serves learning about it will make more sense to you.

Interested Parties

There are various parties who require the accounting information of a business. The list of interested parties includes owners, investors, creditors, governments, management, employees, and even researchers.

Owners

Owners include the proprietors of a sole proprietorship, partners of a firm, and the legal owners of the company or its shareholders. The information provided by accounting records is quintessential for the owners. The owners offer business started with the aim of earning profits. So, they need to have information about the following to steer the business in the right direction.

- A systematic record of earnings,
- All the expenses incurred,
- Any profits earned or losses incurred,
- Amount of capital available,
- Nature and the net value of all the assets owned,
- The quantum of liabilities owed,
- The record of any amount due to suppliers, creditors, or others related to credit purchases,
- Any amount owed by customers or others to the business for the sales of goods or provision of services,
- Accounting information along with facts for filing necessary returns like sales tax returns, income tax returns, all whilst tax returns.

Only when all this information is available to the owners will they be able to make qualified decisions. A businessman might not be able to ascertain the necessary facts about the business if there is no proper system of accounting.

Management team

The management along with the ownership of a sole proprietorship lies with the proprietor himself. However, there are various organizations like body corporate or partnership firms wherein the management and the ownership are different. The management of such businesses as often interested in any information pertaining to the business. They need accounting information for setting targets for the future or the upcoming financial year, for measuring and evaluating the performance of the organization, and for identifying any areas where the business is falling short. Most of the information that they need is a financial nature and will be prepared from accounting records.

Creditors

Every business requires capital for its day-to-day operations. Most of it comes in the form of the capital invested and any loans taken. Creditors include all the parties that provide a business with the necessary goods, raw materials, services, and other financial resources by extending a line of credit or providing loans. Lending companies, financial institutions, banks, and suppliers are all included in the group of creditors. Before providing credit or loan, a creditor will need to determine whether the business is capable of repaying the loan or not. Accounting records, along with financial statements, will help determine the financial health of a business. The common things that a creditor looks for are the business's existing cash position, any outstanding debts, and the current and future earning ability of the business. All this information is provided by the financial records of the business.

Potential investors

An investor would need to carefully analyze the financial position of a business before investing his money in it. A prospective investor often requires a detailed report about the progress of the company, along with its future plans. They require data about the past and the present performance of a business along with any key decisions that will affect the growth of the business in the future. Only after they have all these facts can an investor make an investing decision.

Employees

Just like creditors, even employees need the information associated with the working of a business. Since their livelihood depends upon the performance of the business, they will be interested in understanding its financial health. Most of the labor unions need accounting information of a business to analyze the salary and come up with any fringe benefits.

Governments

Every business is a financial entity and is required to pay certain taxes. It needs to pay federal as well as sales taxes. Governments need a record of the financial statements of a business to ascertain whether a specific concern is paying all its dues or not.

Basic Accounting Principles and Guidelines

If we can understand the accounting principles, we can clearly understand generally accepted accounting principles as it is based on it. Following are the main accounting principles and guidelines.

Economic entity assumption

The accountant has to separate all of the business financial transactions of a sole proprietorship and his personal transactions. But if it is for legal purposes, the business financial transaction and personal transactions of a person is considered as an entity whereas, for accounting purposes, they are separate entities.

According to this concept, every business is supposed to be treated as an entity that is different from its creditors, owners, managers, and other parties. So, the proprietor of an organization or business will always be distinct from the business he controls or owns. In the books of accounts, all the transactions need to be recorded from the perspective of the business and not that of the owner. If the proprietor invests capital in his

39

business, the said capital will be treated as a loan to the business and the owner is a creditor.

The accounting principle of business entity applies to different forms of business organizations. For instance, from a legal perspective, a body corporate is deemed to be a separate entity. While a sole proprietorship along with this business is considered to be a single entity. This perspective changes when it comes to accounting. In accounting, business is considered to be an entity by itself. This is one of the most basic accounting principles, which has been accepted across the world. So, only the transactions associated with the business will be recorded and reported in the books of accounts. Any of the proprietor's personal transactions will not be included. While preparing the books of accounts or the balance sheet, the proprietor's assets and liabilities will not be clubbed with those of the business. The income earned by the business will be different from the income earned by the proprietor.

Monetary unit assumption

All the economic activities are counted in U.S. dollars, and they record transactions that are expressed in U.S. dollars only.

Only all those events or transactions that can be expressed in monetary terms are included in the accounting. Any event that cannot be expressed in monetary terms is excluded even if it affects the earning capacity of an organization. For instance, the working conditions of a company, the sales policy of an enterprise, the capability of the management team, the quality of products produced by a company, will affect the earning capacity. However, all these factors cannot be included in accounting because they cannot be expressed in monetary terms. So, anything that cannot be expressed in dollars will not be included. This concept puts a serious restriction on what can and cannot be recorded. Even though it has certain limitations, this is one of the most important concepts of accounting. It helps to improve one's understanding of and organization's working. Let us assume that a business has a plot of land, 2 tons of raw material, 40 tables, hundred chairs, a cash balance of $7000, and so on. In the absence of this concept, it wouldn't have been possible to include all these assets in the books of accounts. However, if the plot is valued at $30,000, the raw material at $4000 and the furniture at $5000, then all these items can be included as assets in the books of accounts.

A major limitation of this concept is that it doesn't take into consideration the purchasing power of money. The purchasing power of money changes along with time. For instance, if a building was purchased at $20,000 in 1960 and another was purchased in 1974, the same amount. Even if the previous building is worth more now, it will still be accorded at $20,000 in the books of accounts. As the purchasing power of money increases or decreases along with inflation, the value of assets also changes over time. This concept ignores inflation.

Dual aspect concept

This principle is the basis of accountancy. Every business transaction that is recorded in the books of accounts will have a dual aspect. The three important terms of this concept are based on our assets, capital, and creditors. Different writers tend to define asset in different ways. However, a common point to all the definitions is that it is an expenditure for acquiring valuable resources, which benefit the future activities of business. Building, machinery, furniture, inventory, debtors, land, and bills receivable are some of the examples of assets. Without these assets no business can be niche related or sustained. The assets that are business will depend upon the kind of profits it wants to make, and the industries involved in.

No business can run without assets. Now, the question arises where these assets are opting. One source of assets is the capital invested in business. The proprietor of the owner of a business invests his funds in the business in the form of capital. The amount of assets that are business has to be equally proportional to the amount of capital that the investor has. In other words, it can be said that when the proprietor puts his money in the business, this transaction gives rise to two effects; the assets of the business increase and the claim of the proprietor is also recognized. Since the system of thinking gives rise to two aspects, it is known as the dual aspect concept of the double entry system. In this case, the above event can be easily expressed as capital = assets.

In case the capital contributed by the proprietor is insufficient for a business to take off, then the business can borrow from others. All those who lend money to the business or give it some credit facilities are known as creditors. When you from the point of view of a business, each of these events also gives rise to two effects. On one hand, the loan obtained by the business will increase its assets and on the other, the claim of the creditor will also increase in the business. To sum up all the points up until now, capital + liabilities = assets.

Time period assumption

The net income of a business can be measured by comparing its assets from the time of its commencement to the date of liquidation. Since accounting is based on the concept that the business will go on for an indefinite period of time, measuring income using the above principle is not prudent. It is impractical for a business to fade for prolonged periods traded mine its net income. This is where the concept of accounting period comes in. If a business tries to measure its income from its conception to liquidation, you cannot determine whether the business is doing good or bad. To calculate its profitability, it is quintessential bad financial statements from time to time. Only when the financial statements are prepared can any corrective actions be taken. For instance, if for one quarter, a business has sustained significant losses, then corrective measures cannot be implemented without financial statements.

This principle states that in a short period of time, the company's complex and ongoing business activities can be reported with accuracy, for example, the five months ended May 31, 2019, or the five weeks ended May 1. 2019. When the time period is shorter, the accountant needs to assume the relevant amount in that short period. Suppose, the tax bill of the property is issued on December 15 every year so, the amount in the income statement in December end 2018 is known but the income statement in three months ending on May 31, 2019, is unknown, so the accountant has to estimate the amount.

It is very important to mention the time interval in the heading of every income statement, stockholder's equity statements, and statement of cash flows. One cannot label December 31 in these income statements. The reader should know if it is one week ended December 31, 2019, the month ended December 2019, three months ended December 2019, or the year ended December 2019.

Cost principle

For an accountant, the word 'cost' means the money spent on an object when it was bought, despite its purchase time. This is the reason that the amounts in the financial statements are called historical cost amounts. There are two assumptions upon which the cost concept is based. The first assumption is that all the records will be recorded in the books of accounts at the price for which they were acquired. The second assumption is that the same cost will be used for any subsequent accounting related to the said asset. Whenever an asset is acquired, its net value tends to change over time. However, this change in net assets value is not considered while using the cost concept. For instance, if a piece of equipment was purchased for $8000, then it will be reflected in the final accounts as $8000 even if the market value is $7500. When a balance sheet is prepared based on the cost concept, it will not usually include the fluctuations in the net value of an asset.

If a business doesn't pay anything to acquire an asset, it will not show up in the books of accounts. So, if the business has any goodwill, it cannot be shown in the books of accounts since the company hasn't paid a penny to acquire it — objectivity and feasibility either to concepts which guide accounting activity. However, the cost principle fails to consider relevance while preparing accounts. At times, it isn't objective to try and estimate the market value of every asset given the fluctuations. The cost concept makes it more feasible. This concept doesn't help investors or other users because it usually shows the historical cost of the asset and not the existing cost. By following this concept, and the accountant is sacrificing relevancy for obtaining better feasibility and objectivity.

The company's asset is not changed or altered in regard to inflation because of this principle. The general rule is that an asset's value will not be changed to show any type of value increase. This is why the asset amount will not show the money that a company will get if it sells the asset in current markets value. There is an exception in some investments in stocks and bonds that are traded in the stock market. So, we cannot find a company's long-term asset value in the company's financial statements. A third party can do this job.

Full disclosure principle

Certain information is a must for the investors or lenders to know. So, this information should be mentioned in the financial statements or the notes attached to the financial statements. This principle is the reason behind many pages of 'footnotes' attached with financial statements.

The concept of full disclosure primarily implies that the accounts of a company need to be prepared honestly. It doesn't mean that all information needs to be disclosed, but sufficient information that can influence the interest of proprietors along with creditors and investors need to be disclosed. For instance, if a business has any contingent liabilities, they need to be showcased in the financial statements in the form of a footnote. For example, if a company is in a lawsuit and owes a lot of money when the financial statement is prepared, it is not sure if the company will win the case or end up losing money to the lawsuit, it's not clear so the lawsuit will be clearly mentioned in the financial statement.

Going concern principle

The going concern concept has been defined by Kohler's dictionary for accounting, as the assumption that a final indefinite period. It is based on the assumption that a business is not going to be liquidated any time soon. Indefinite existence means that a specific organization or business will not be liquidated in the foreseeable future. This essentially means that the concerned business is going to be able to meet any of its financial concerns and goals. The concept of liquidation is based on this principle. Fixed asset will appreciate its value over time. For instance, if a piece of equipment is acquired by a business and its expected lifetime is five years, then the total cost of acquisition of such a machine will be asserted for a period of five years while calculating the business's income.

In this accounting principle, the accountant can assume whether the company is going to prosper and achieve its motives and goals or not. If the accountant feels that the financial statement of the company shows or signals its liquidation, the assessment has to be disclosed clearly. This principle allows the company to defer a few of the prepaid expenses until the upcoming accounting period.

Matching principle

The most important factor that ensures that a proprietor will stay interested in his business is his desire to earn profits. Therefore, it is but obvious that an accountant's primary focus must be to improve the techniques for measuring income. An accountant's job is not just to calculate the revenue earned but must also calculate the expenses that have been incurred. There are two aspects of the matching concept, and they are the revenue realization concept and the matching costs. The first step to applying the principle of matching is to determine the period within which the revenue is realized. Revenue can be realized on the basis of sales, cash, or production. If revenue is recognized on sales basis, income will be recorded only when a sale is complete. A sale is completed when assets have been transferred to the buyer in exchange for a payment. Only when cash has received upon the realization of a sale will it be recorded in the books of accounts when the cash concept is followed. Revenue will be realized only when the production is completed when a business follows the concept of production bases. According to the completion of the work, the costs involved will be determined. For instance, a contract assigned to a construction job might require two years are the completion of the project. At such times, the contractor has the option of calculating his revenue and earnings from the project based on a percentage of completion. The second aspect of the matching concept is the matching of cost. Whenever the income from the business operation is being calculated, the course that was incurred while earning the revenue needs to be included. So, certain costs like from the sale of capital assets, loss incurred due to an accident, and other causes even though not related to the regular business operations need to be included while calculating the revenue. Anything which leads to cash flow from the business must be included.

In this, the accounting principle, the accrual basis of accounting is applied. The matching principle states that expenses have to match with the revenues. For example, the commission expenses should be mentioned when sales were made, and not when commissions are paid. The employ wages should be reported when the employees are working and not when the wages are given. So, if a company is going to pay 1% of 2019 sales to their employees on January 15, 2020, it should be mentioned as an expense in 2019 and the amount unpaid in 2020 as a liability. Since the advertisements benefit cannot be confirmed, the ad expenditure is out in as an expense until the ad is running.

Revenue recognition principle

According to the revenue recognition concept, there are two things that must be considered. The first aspect is that a transaction will only be recognized whenever there is an inflow or outflow of funds. The second aspect is that revenue must be recognized at the point of sale while keeping consideration of any gains or losses that were incurred during the course of the transaction. According to revenue recognition concept, revenue can be realized by the business only when the goods or services produced by it are transferred to the customer either for some asset, cash or for some promise to pay the cash in future. This is closely related to the legal principle related to the transfer of any property. Revenue must be recognized only when the business actually sells something to the customer. For instance, if a business receives an order to supply goods in June in the month of March, then the sale will be realized only June. This concept is quite important because it prevents businesses from inflating their incomes or profits by recording any future sales. Transactions need to be recorded only when they are finalized, and the payment has been received.

This principle also follows the accrual basis of accounting and not cash basis of accounting. So, in this principle, revenue is considered right after the product is sold off or the service is performed, if the money is received is not taken into consideration. So, in this principle, a company can report almost $30000 revenue and still have $0 in their account in that month.

Suppose, if Vogue has agreed to post an ad for 3000$, Vogue can report $3000 right after signing the deal even if the money is transferred after 30 days. So, revenue and cash receipts should never be confused.

Materiality

It is the accountant's duty to make an objective distinction between transactions that can be considered to be material or immaterial. If an accountant fails to make this distinction, then the accounting process will be unnecessarily overburdened by several minute details that don't add any value. According to the American Accounting Association materiality is defined as follows.

An item is considered to be material when there is a reason to believe that its presence or its knowledge will influence the decision of an investor or other interested parties. If anything can influence the judgment of a prudent man, then it is considered to be a material transaction. At times are certain unimportant items which are left out of financial statements are merged with other items. These items can be either shown as footnotes or in parentheses based on their importance. For instance, the amount of profit or loss shown in the profit and loss account can change because of a change in the business's accounting practice. Any change in the calculation of depreciation will influence the profit or loss incurred on the sale of the assets. If it is believed that this information will not influence and interested party's decision, then it doesn't have to be included in the business accounts. All such information must be disclosed, which can affect the decision of existing or potential investors.

Conservatism

The principle of conservatism is based on the idea of playing safe. While following this concept, a business takes into consideration all losses while understating any prospective profits. By following this concept, and the accountant will record all unfavorable events that can affect the value of an asset, owner's equity, and income. The least favorable effects are immediately recorded while leaving out any prospective profits. For instance, any provision that is made for doubtful debts or any discount given to debtors will be included by following this concept. Any provision created for fluctuations in the price of assets or investments like depreciation will be recorded during the following conservatism. Along with that, amortization of intangible assets will also be included. This concept is usually applied whenever that happens to be any uncertainty regarding an activity. An inherent uncertainty can be about incurring a loss, an estimated liability, or even the useful life of an asset. By following this concept, and the accountant has the option of choosing a conservative approach when there are two acceptable methods of accounting involved. Whenever there happens to be a possibility of incurring a loss of earning a profit, then the profits will be overlooked while the loss will be accounted for. By doing this, it enables a business to prepare itself any potential losses.

This conservatism principle helps the accountant when in a dilemma with two acceptable alternatives in mentioning an item. So, this principle allows the accountant to choose the option in which the end result will lead to less asset amount and/or less net income. This principle doesn't allow the accountants to be conservative. The accountants are supposed to be completely unbiased and practical.

So, this conservatism principle will allow accountants to mention down losses and not the gains. For example, if a company loses a case in a lawsuit, the accountants will mention it, but if it gains extra in the case, they are not going to mention it. However, this concept needs to be used cautiously. If this principle is used without any restrictions, it leads to the creation of secret reserves, which will be in direct contradiction of the full disclosure principle. The idea is to enable the business to fortify itself from any losses. So, it must not be misused to deceive other parties involved in the business.

Other Characteristics of Accounting Information

Following are the characteristics of accounting information when a professional accountant provides the accounting information:

- It should be reliable, verifiable, and objective.
- There should be consistency
- Accounting information should have comparability

Reliable, Verifiable, and Objective

Not only should a piece of accounting information follow all the above-mentioned accounting principles and guidelines, but should also be reliable, verifiable, and objective.

This concept means that all the accounting transactions must be evidenced and supported by business documents. The supporting documents include invoices, correspondence, and so on. The supporting documents provide the basis for making accounting entries and for verification of the same by auditors. The evidence of stands in the business transaction must be objective evidence. It essentially means that the evidence should support packs as they are without any bias toward either side. This concept forms the basis of auditing.

Suppose, if the mentioned says a land purchased 50 years ago at $ 60000, it looks more reliable, verifiable, and objective than the current price value of $ 400,000. If the original cost is given to many different accountants, all of them will come to one conclusion about the original cost based on the offer and acceptance, transfer tax and the documents. But if the current market price value is given to them, all of them will come out with a different end result. It therefore becomes unreliable, unverifiable, and not very objective.

Accounting principle has nodded to move away with the cost principle if the amounts are reliable, verifiable, and objective. For example, if a company has bought a stock, and the stock is currently traded in the stock exchange, the company has to show the current rate instead of the original bought value. The one limitation of this concept is that it isn't possible to verify every single entry that is made. Certain steps can be taken to ensure that all the data entered is true and fair, but 100% accuracy cannot be guaranteed when humans are involved.

Consistency

The accountants of the company have to be consistent in applying accounting principles, methods, and practices. Accounting practices, as well as concepts, need to be practiced consistently. If the management is to draw any important conclusions about the effectiveness of the business, there needs to be consistency. If the methods keep changing from one accounting period to another, it becomes difficult to compare the performance of the business. Consistency doesn't mean rigidity. New techniques of accounting can be introduced, but they need to be used consistently.

The principle of consistency comes in handy whenever there are various methods of accounting that can be used for a particular transaction. For instance, depreciation will be charged over the lifetime of a fixed asset. However, when it comes to calculating depreciation, there are several methods available. Businesses are free to charge depreciation according to any of these methods. If the business decides to charge depreciation according to the straight-line method and needs to ensure that the method of depreciation will be followed over the course of the life of an asset, if the method keeps changing from one accounting period to another, it will become very difficult to assert on the net value of the asset.

If a company has been using the FIFO cost flow assumption, the financial statement readers will expect the company to be using it. If the company switches to using the LIFO cost flow assumption, the accountant should mention it clearly in the financial statement.

Comparability

If it is in the same type of industry, investors, shareholders, and other users expect that the financial statement of one company can be compared to the financial statement of the other company. Comparability between different financial statements of many companies is one feature of Generally Accepted Accounting principles.

Financial Reporting

The disclosure of a company's performance in finance and other related information over a certain period of time to the management and external stakeholders like an investor, customer, and regulators is called financial reporting.

The financial reports are issues either quarterly or annually and consist of the following:

- Balance Sheet or Statement of Financial Position – this consist of a company's assets, liabilities, and owner's equity at a given time, which is usually the fiscal quarter or year.
- Income Statement or Profit and Loss Report – this consist of the income, expenses, and profits of a company over a certain period of

time, usually the fiscal quarter or year. So, this comprises of the total sales and many expenses done during that given period of time.

- Statement of Changes in Equity or Statement of Retained Earnings – it mentions the equity changes of a company during the given time period usually the fiscal quarter or year.
- Cash Flow Statement – this consist of the cash flow activities in the company, which includes, operating, investing, and financing activities. These are called as sources and uses of cash.

These financial reports will be very detailed and complex in publicly held corporations. They usually add extensive footnotes, and along with that, they include a management discussion and analysis (MD&A). These footnotes provide detailed information about each item listed on the balance sheet, income statement, and cash flow statements. These notes also include the type of method used for preparing the accounting report.

The private and public companies have to follow generally accepted accounting guidelines (GAAP) while preparing their financial reports. U.S. companies have to report under the U.S. generally accepted accounting guidelines (GAAP), and the other international companies have to report under International Financial Reporting Standards (IFRS). When the accounting principles and guidelines are followed in accounting, it assures accuracy, consistency, and comparability in the financial report.

Cash Basis Accounting vs. Accrual Accounting

The main differentiating fact between cash and accrual accounting is the timing of the sales and purchases recorded in the accounts.

Cash basis accounting only records revenue and expenses only when the money is received in the account, whereas in accrual basis accounting, revenue is considered as soon as it is earned, and the expenses billed.

Cash basis accounting

In cash basis accounting, revenues are taken into consideration only when it is received, and the expenses are considered only when the bill is paid. This method of accounting does not consider the accounts that will be received or paid later.

Most of the small-scale businesses choose this method of accounting because it is very simple and easy to regulate. It is very easy to track when a transaction is done and if the money has been deposited or sent from a bank account. There is no need to keep track of the accounts that are to be received or paid.

This cash basis accounting method is also very beneficial in checking the company's current bank account balance at any given time and checks the resources of the money.

And since the transaction is not recorded until the money is in the bank account, the business income tax is not taxed unless it's in your bank account.

Accrual basis accounting

In this accrual basis accounting method, the revenues and expenses are noted and recorded immediately when they are earned or billed, regardless of whether the money is actually received or paid. For instance, a company will add the revenue right after completion of a project rather than waiting for the payment to be received. This method is used and followed more than the cash basis accounting method. Normally, all transactions are settled in cash but even if settlement of cash has not yet taken place, it is justified to include the transaction are the events related to the books of accounts. The accrual concept recognizes revenue when it is earned rather than when it is collected and recognizes expenses when assets or the benefits are used rather than when they are paid for. The financial statements might not reveal the true and fair view of the affairs of a business unit undersold the transactions are events related to a particular year are entered into the books of accounts. So, by following the accrual basis of accounting, this can be done.

This accrual basis accounting method provides a better view or sight of a company's income and expenses, so it gives better information about the company's future business conditions. Cash basis accounting cannot do this.

The main disadvantage of this accrual basis accounting is that the actual cash flow is not at all informed. So even though a company might be making a lot of money in accrual accounting but in reality, can be out of money in a bank account so it is very important to keep track of bank account or cash flow also the end result can be disappointing.

The effects of cash and accrual accounting

It is very important and moreover mandatory to know the difference between cash basis accounting and accrual basis accounting when you start a business. And also, you have to see the effects of each of these accounting methods.

These are the ways each cash and accrual basis accounting effects:

Suppose you do the following transactions in a month of business:

- Sent an invoice of $7000 for a web design project that was completed this month.
- Received $3000 for developing a website this month.

- Gave $300 in fees for a bill, which you got last month.

- Received $3000 from a client for a work given last month.

The effect on cash flow

If we use the cash basis accounting method, the total profit of this month will be $ 2700 ($3,000 income minus $300 fees).

If we use the accrual accounting method, the total profit of this month will be $4,000 ($7,000 income minus $3,000 developer fees).

The above example shows that the two different accounting methods can lead to different accounting of profits and cash flow. So, the choice of accounting method does make a huge difference.

The effect on taxes

Suppose we consider that the above-given example happened in between November and December 2018. One of the main differences between the two accounting methods is that they have a huge impact on the business tax depending on the time the income and expenses are recorded,

If we use cash basis accounting, the income is only recorded when the cash is received in the bank account, whereas if we use accrual basis accounting, it is recorded right after it is earned.

So, if we follow the accrual basis accounting, if the invoice for $7000 was confirmed on December 2018, it will be recorded as a transaction done in 2018 and pay income tax for it even if you receive the cash in January 2019.

Types of Accounts

An account is often referred to as the formal record of a specific type of transaction that is expressed in monetary terms. When it comes to the double-entry system, every transaction has a twofold effect. Therefore, there are two accounts that are involved. One account will be debited, whereas the other will be credited. For the purposes of accounting, every transaction made bad business can be classified into three categories.

- The transactions that are relating to individuals are persons.
- The transactions relating to property, possession, or assets.
- The transactions relating to incomes and other expenses.

Corresponding to the three categories of transactions that were mentioned above, the following three classes of accounts are prepared for recording all the business transactions.

- Personal accounts.
- Real or property accounts.
- Nominal accounts.

Now, let us look in detail about each of these three types of accounts. It is quintessential to learn about these accounts because the basic rules of debit and credit are based on it.

A personal account is used for recording any dealings of a trader or a business with other persons of forms. A separate account will be opened for each such person, performed for recording the transactions. The account of each person at the firms will be debited with any benefit such a person or firm receives and is credited with any benefit that such a person or firm provides. Personal accounts are further classified into the following.

Natural person's account

For instance, includes supplier's accounts, receiver's accounts, and proprietor's accounts.

Artificial person's accounts or body of person's accounts: For instance, any bank account, insurance company's accounts, government's account, and any limited company's account.

Representative personal accounts: Includes any account that's used for representing a particular person or persons. For instance, if a business cannot pay the salaries to its employees, then the account created in the books of the business would be Salaries Outstanding Account.

Real accounts

Real accounts are also referred to as property accounts, and the record any transactions related to property, assets and possessions of business. All those items, which are more or less permanent, are recorded in the real accounts. A separate account is maintained for each class of property or possession owned by the business such as stock of goods, equipment, furniture and fixtures, cash, machinery, and so on. In each of these accounts, the particular is related to that asset are maintained. It helps a business to identify the net value of each of its assets on a given date. Real accounts are classified into tangible real accounts and intangible real accounts. Tangible real accounts include all tangible assets like land, cash account, stock account, furniture account, building account, and so on. Intangible accounts include trademarks, patents rights, and goodwill accounts. These accounts include all such things that are difficult to touch in the physical sense but are capable of being measured and pecuniary value.

Nominal accounts

Fictitious accounts or nominal accounts are these accounts are used for defining the nature of transactions. These accounts are used for recording any losses or gains of a business. Here is an example to make things clear. If an employee gets his salary, and the agent gets his commission, a worker gets his wages; a lender gets interest on money, all dealings are made in cash. Cash is the real thing that exists, and salary, commission, interest, wages, and other terms are used for merely describing the nature of the transaction for which the cash was used. If nominal accounts didn't exist, it would become rather difficult to keep track of all essential business transactions.

Rules for Double-Entry

Now that you're aware of all the different types of accounts, it is time to learn about the double-entry system. The double entry system basically provides the rules of debit and credit. Every transaction has two aspects - an incoming aspect (debit) and an outgoing aspect (credit). The rules of the double-entry system are based on these two aspects. Since there are three types of accounts, there are three rules for recording all the transactions in the respective accounts.

Rules for personal account

The person account holders receive something from the business will be debited while the person's account who give something to the business will be credited. If ABC gives $2000 to the business, then it is said that ABC's account will be credited.

Rules for real account

All the assets that are acquired by the business will be debited, and all those that go are the business will be credited. For instance, if business purchases are building for $ 100,000 in cash, then the building's account will be debited, and the cash account will be credited.

Rules for expenses and incomes

All expenses and losses will be debited while all incomes and games will be credited. For instance, if the rent is paid by a business, then the rent account will be debited while the cash account will be credited.

Chapter Four: Recording Transactions

When the transactions of a company are recorded in the general ledger accounts, it is called bookkeeping. This term is usually used to refer to any accounting task that is carried out before preparing the trial balance.

Different people will think of bookkeeping in different ways:

There are people who think of bookkeeping as accounting itself. They will assume that everything some keeping the company's books to preparing tax reports is included in bookkeeping.

There are those who see it as just recording transactions in a journal or diary. The amounts are then entering into the accounts in the ledger. This signifies the end of bookkeeping for them; a real accountant then handles the work.

Using computers and advanced accounting software has blurred the lines that differentiated bookkeeping and accounting. Even someone with basic training in bookkeeping can use accounting software. The software will automatically update general ledger accounts after the records are entered. After establishing the financial statement format, this software can generate financial statements too.

Bookkeeping is not a term that is used in larger corporations anymore. Such organizations usually have a whole department that is dedicated to accounting and staffed with well-trained accountants.

You have to understand the relationship of bookkeeping with accounting. There is some confusion over the distinction between bookkeeping and accounting. This is due in part to the fact that the two are related and that there is no universally accepted line, which demarcates them. Usually, bookkeeping is the art of maintaining or keeping the accounts in a prescribed manner. Accounts are maintained for registering for noting the facts of transactions in a clear and understandable manner. Most of the work related to bookkeeping is clerical in nature. Accounting is mainly concerned with the design of the system of records, preparation of reports based on the recorded data, and the interpretation of the report. Accountants often direct and review the work of keepers. Bookkeeping is an activity that is complementary to the process of accounting. Accounting develops information for providing answers to the following questions.

How good or bad is the financial condition of the business? Have the operations of the business of the whole resulted in a profit or loss? How have the different functions of the department performed? And how successful have been the results of individual activities of products? What are the likely results of new decisions to be made or old decisions that may be modified? In the light of the past results of operations, how must the business enterprise planned activities attain the expected results?

Accounting and bookkeeping will involve recording financial transactions of the company. These transactions are to be identified, approved, and sorted so that they can be retrieved when needed and presented in financial statements of the company.

The following are some examples of financial transactions of a consonant:

- Using cash to purchase supplies
- Using the credit to purchase merchandise
- Using credit for the sale of merchandise
- Rent for business office
- The wages and salaries of employees
- Buying equipment for office
- Borrowing from banks

All of these transactions will be sorted into accounts, and the amounts that are in each account will be reported in the financial statements of the company. This may be in a summary form or in detail. There may be hundreds of accounts and an even greater number of transactions. This will allow more efficiency and information that will help to manage the business better.

Since there is sophisticated accounting software available now, it is impractical to use manual accounting for a business. A minimum amount of data entry is required for the software to do all the work for accounting. One of the most popularly used accounting software is QuickBooks.

Why are Debits and Credits Important?

The terms debit and credit have actually been used for hundreds of years and are not as modern as they might sound.

The double entry system will require every transaction to be recorded in two accounts. The first account will receive an entry of debit, and this entry will be done on the left side. The other account will receive an entry of credit, and this will be done on the right side. Initially, in double entry, it may be confusing to decide which account has to be debited and which account credited.

Debiting an account means making entries on the left side of that account. Crediting an account will mean making entries on the right side of that account. Abbreviation for debit is dr. and the abbreviation for credit is cr.

The following types of accounts are usually increased with debits:

- Dividends
- Assets
- Expenses
- Losses

The following account types are usually increased with credits:

- Gains
- Income
- Revenues
- Liabilities
- Stockholders equity

To decrease account on one side, opposite of what was done to increase will have to be done. If a debit increases an account, a credit can be used to decrease the account.

Journal Entries

The term journal entry comes from the fact that in manual accounting, business transactions are first recorded in journals.

The journal entries in the general journal of a company will contain the following information:

- The correct dates
- The account that will be debited
- The amount that will be debited

- The account that will be credited
- The amount that will be credited
- A short reference

Journal entries in the journal will be entered according to dates, and then they are entered in their appropriate accounts of the general ledger.

The journals are referred to as the book of verse or original entry. Since all transactions are first recorded in the journals before they are transferred to any of accounts. The journal provides a chronological order of all the transactions made by the business. It shows the date wage transaction along with the amount sought the accounts that have to be debited or credited. Journals also often provide a brief explanation of the transaction involved. Every business transaction can be recorded in a simple journal. A business deal can also record specific transactions in different books of accounts known as special journals. Special journals include Sales Journal for any credit sales, Purchases Journal for any credit purchases, Purchases Returns Journals, and so on. Journals are created on the basis of the double-entry system of accounting. So, every transaction made by the business has two effects. Let us look at a couple of transactions to get a better idea of how journal entries are made. For instance, ABC starts a business with $ 50,000, and the capital is in the form of cash. So, the journal entry for this transaction would be as follows.

Cash A/c Dr. ---------------- $50,000

To ABC's A/c ---------------- $50,000.

(Being money invested in the business)

If $4000 is paid as rent by the business, then the transaction will be recorded as follows.

Rent A/c Dr. ---------------- $4,000

To Cash A/c ---------------- $4,000.

(Being rent paid in cash)

In computerized accounting, business transactions will be recorded automatically into the general ledger. This is why journal entries are not written for most business transactions now.

However, despite using computerized accounting, some journal entries still have to be made. This includes the adjusting entries.

General Ledger

A general ledger will be a grouping of accounts that are used for sorting and storing information from the business transactions of a company. It will be organized as balance sheet accounts and income statement accounts. The balance sheet accounts will include equity, assets, and liabilities. The income statement accounts will include gains, losses, expenses, and revenues.

If you use the double-entry accounting system, every transaction made will affect two or more than two general ledger accounts. The debit amount of every transaction has to be equal to the credit amount. This is why the general ledger should have an equal number of debits and credits. When totaled, the account balances that are listed on trial balance should be equal.

In the case of manual accounting, general ledgers are usually books where there is a separate page kept for every account. A subsidiary ledger is used if a lot of information is required for an account. In computerized accounting, the general ledger will be in the form of an electronic file that has all the required accounts. This helps to facilitate electronic preparation of the financial statements of the company.

What is a general ledger account?

It is an account that is used for sorting, storing, and summarizing the transactions of a company. The accounts will be arranged in the general ledger. The balance sheet accounts come first, and then the income statement accounts.

Balance sheet accounts will usually be arranged like the following in a general ledger:

- Asset accounts, like inventory, accounts receivable, and cash.
- Liability accounts like customer deposits, notes payable, and accounts payable.
- Stockholders equity accounts like treasury stock and common stock.
- Income statement accounts will be arranged as:
- Operating revenue accounts, like sales fee revenues.
- Operating expense accounts like rent expense.
- Non-operating accounts like interest expense.

Subsidiary Ledgers

Subsidiary ledgers are often prepared in addition to a general ledger. These are used to record details related to accounts receivable along with Accounts Payable. If there are thousands of customers and numerous credit sales transactions can become quite cumbersome to record them in the general ledger under the heading accounts receivable. It becomes impossible to a certain quantum of the amount receivable from a specific buyer. It also becomes equally difficult to calculate the amount that is owed by a specific customer if the records are maintained only in a general ledger under the heading accounts payable. Instead of this system, a subsidiary ledger is maintained to specifically a certain the amount receivable from an individual director along with the amount that payable to an individual creditor.

A group of accounts maintained in this fashion is known as subsidiary ledgers. When these ledgers maintained, it is not required to maintain a detailed account of the accounts receivable or payable on the general ledger. There are two types of common subsidiary ledgers maintained by any business- the accounts receivable subsidiary ledger and the Accounts Payable subsidiary ledger. The data in these ledgers maintained in alphabetical order. The data from subsidiary ledgers is briefly recorded in certain accounts of the general ledger, and they are known as the control ledgers. At the end of an accounting period, the total of each subsidiary ledger will be equal to the balance of every control account. For instance, the balance of accounts payable in the general ledger will be equal to the total balances of all the individual accounts maintained in the Accounts Payable subsidiary ledger.

Let us look at an example to understand this relationship.

X

Date	Account title	Ref	Debit	Credit	Balance
2019			$	$	$
Feb 2	Sales		12,000		12,000
Feb 15	Cash			8,000	4,000

Y

ACCOUNTING

Date	Account title	Ref	Debit	Credit	Balance
2019			$	$	$
Feb 12	Sales		6,000		6,000
Feb 21	Cash			6,000	Nil

Z

Date	Account title	Ref	Debit	Credit	Balance
2019			$	$	$
Feb 20	Sales		6,000		6,000
Feb 25	Cash			2,000	4,000

General Ledger- Accounts Receivable

Date	Account title	Ref	Debit	Credit	Balance
2019			$	$	$
Feb 28	Sales		24,000		24,000
Feb 28	Cash			16,000	8,000

The balance of the accounts receivable in the general balance is $8000 and this amount is equivalent to the summation of the individual ledgers mentioned in the subsidiary ledger. The balance of the control account mentioned in the general ledger will always be equal to the total of the balances mentioned in the concerned in which ledger accounts. If these balances are equal, then it shows an error in the books of accounts.

ACCOUNTING

Here are the reasons why a business will use subsidiary journalists instead of maintaining just one general journal.

All transactions of a similar nature will be collected in one place. For instance, all the credit sales recorded in the sales book. This, in turn, helps to post any impersonal accounts along with the balances.

It also helps with the division of responsibilities. For instance, the posting of a certain ledger can be entrusted to different workers at the same time. Therefore, the accounts of a large company can be written up quickly. It also helps to introduce internal checks.

Whenever entries are recorded in the subsidiary journals, enables a business to record more details that cannot be included in a general ledger.

Whenever transactions of a similar nature are collected in one place, it enables the accountant to perform a careful survey of any trend, pattern of distribution, and other helpful. All this information in handy while making any day-to-day decisions about the operation of a business. For instance, a careful analysis of those sales return ledger can help understand the cause of such returns along with any loss sustained in this process.

Trial Balance

Trial balance is a report of bookkeeping or accounting that will list out the balances in all the general ledger accounts of an organization. There will be a column labeled as "debit balances" and the debit balance amounts are listed here. Another column labeled "credit balances" will have a list of all the credit balance accounts. When the total is calculated for each column, they should be the same.

Once all the accounts have been balanced off, they are placed in a list with credit balances on one side and debit balances on the other. This list is referred to as a trial balance. Since most of the accounting records are based on the double entry system, the trial balance needs to tally. If the totals on both sides current arithmetically correct, then must be some error in the preparation of the books of accounts. However, just because the balances tally doesn't mean that the trial balance is free of all errors. Here are the main characteristics of a trial balance.

- This statement is prepared in a tabular form. It consists of two columns, one for credit balances and the other foot debit balances.
- The balances obtained from a ledger account for the closing balances are shown in the trial balance.

- The trial balance is not a statement and account per se and is merely a statement of all balances.
- As long as the ledger accounts are balanced, trial balance can be prepared whenever required.
- It provides a consolidated list of the ledger balances at the end of a given period.
- Trial balance is used for checking the arithmetical accuracy of all the ledger accounts.
- Trial balance is used for creating other financial statements like profit and loss account, trading account, and the balance sheet as well.
- Here are the reasons why a trial balance is usually prepared.
- The first reason is that it has strictly arithmetical accuracy of the books of accounts.
- If there is any error while creating the subsidiary books or records, it will be immediately reflected in the trial balance.
- If there is any error in the posting of entries to the subsidiary books, even that can be easily figured out.
- A trial balance makes it easier to verify the schedules of debtors as well as creditors.
- Any error regarding balancing of accounts can also be checked using the trial balance.

Limitations of a trial balance

Keep in mind that a trial balance is never conclusive proof of accuracy of the books of accounts. Even if the trial balance tallies, it doesn't necessarily mean that the books of accounts are free of all errors. There are some errors that remain undetected or undisclosed while preparing a trial balance. This is perhaps the major limitation of this statement. In this section, let us look at certain errors that are disclosed by trial balance.

If an entry has been omitted from the original book of records, then it will not reflect on the trial balance. Since both the aspects of a transaction have been completely left off the books of accounts, it will never make it to the trial balance. According to the system of double entry, every transaction needs to have a credit as well as debit aspect to it. Because both of these aspects have never made it to the original book of records, this error will be left undetected. For instance, if goats were sold to ABC on credit, and this fact was never included in the sales journal, it will neither appear on the debit side of ABCs account not the credit side of the sales account.

If an item has been posted to the correct side bar to the wrong account, even then it will not appear in the trial balance for instance if cash was received from ABC but this transaction has been wrongly credited to XYZ instead of ABC's account, even if the amount is correct, there will be no imbalance in the trial balance.

Another error that is left undetected by trial balance is one wrong amount has been entered in the subsidiary books of accounts. For instance, a credit purchase of $4000 was wrongly entered in the purchases book as $400; the error will not show up in the trial balance.

All sorts of compensating errors will not be reflected in the trial balance. For instance, any amount of excess debit or under debit of an account can be neutralized if there is excess credit or under credit to the same quantum on other accounts. This isn't a usual occurrence, but if the amounts compensate for each other, it will never show up on the trial balance. For instance, if an accountant forgets to post $1000 to the debit side of a specific account and then under-posts $1000 to the credit side of another account, the trial balance will tally.

Any error caused due to a wrongly applied principle of accounting will not show up in the trial balance. Whenever a specific amount isn't properly allocated between revenue and capital or whenever a principle of double entry is violated, it is referred to as an error of principle. For instance, if salaries paid to employees are debited to the salaries account, it is an error of principle. Likewise, if the proprietor of a sole proprietorship with straws any goods for personal use, it needs to be debited to the Drawings account and simultaneously credited to the Purchases account.

Preparing a trial balance

A trial balance is not the same as a financial statement. It is more of an internal report that was helpful when manual accounting was done. An imbalance in the trial balance will indicate errors somewhere between the trial balance and journal. This error is usually because of some miscalculation in account balance, posting credit amounts as debit, etc. The accounting software used in the current day has eliminated the chances of such errors. This is why trial balance is not as important as it once was. Now the trial balance and general ledger will quite surely have balanced debits and credits. Auditors and accountants still find trial balance useful in some ways.

Trial balance will have the following information:

- Titles of every general ledger account with a balance
- Two columns on the right of the account titles that will be labeled as debit and credit.
- Every account balance will be listed in the appropriate columns.
- Summary of every column after all the account balances are entered.
- Equal total on the debit column and credit column.

Chapter Five: Financial Statements

What Is A Financial Statement?

Money is often invested in a business to earn profits. To a certain this, it is quintessential that an accountant needs to measure and accurate accounting data in a systematic manner so that the amount of profit on or the loss incurred by the business can be determined as well as reported. It is important to a certain the profits earned to calculate income tax, dividends, and for preparing any future plans of expansion. To determine the profit earned a loss incurred, a statement known as the income statement is prepared. All the items regarding expenses and losses along with revenues and gains occurring within an accounting period are included in the income statement. There is another statement that is prepared to understand the financial position of a business on the last date of the accounting period known as the balance sheet. All these statements together are known as financial statements. They're also referred to as the final accounts of a company because there often calculated at the end of the financial accounting process. The information in these statements comes from the balances appearing in the trial balance.

ACCOUNTING

A financial statement is a systematic and written record related to the business activities along with the financial performance of the company. The income statement concentrates on the revenues and expenses of a company during a specific period. When the expenses are subtracted from the total revenue earned by a company, it produces a figure known as the net income. The balance sheet gives an overview of all the liabilities, assets, and stockholder's equity for a given timeframe. The cash flow statement helps to analyze whether the company has sufficient cash to meet its debt obligations, funding its investments, and managing its operating expenses.

Well, there are certain limitations applicable to the financial statements as well. They certainly provide a lot of information, but these statements are open to interpretation. The way an investor interprets this financial data can vary from one person to another. For instance, an investor might be looking to see whether a company has repurchased the stalks or not while another one might prefer to see that the company is investing money in long-term assets. One investor might be fine with the existing debt level of a company, whereas another in Best might be concerned about the company's debt levels.

Five financial statements should be included when a corporation distributed its annual statements. These are:

- Income statement
- Statement of comprehensive income
- Balance sheet
- Statement of stockholder's equity
- Cash flow statement

Notes to the financial statements also have to be included with these. The notes are used to disclose information about undisclosed amounts that are important but not in the financial statement.

When distributing financial statements, the company has to comply with the generally accepted accounting principles or GAAP rules. The majority of amounts in the financial statements will be from the records of past transactions. This is why these amounts may not always be relevant to future decision-making and cannot indicate what the current fair market value of the company is.

Where do the amounts come from?

The amounts that are reported in financial statements will generally originate from the companies recorded and stored business transactions in their general ledger books. It is to be noted that Accounting records are usually referred to as books.

Accountants record not only business transactions but also the adjusting entries. Adjusting entries are important for various reasons, including:

Certain recorded transaction amounts may pertain to more than a single accounting period. This accounting period could be weeks, months, years, etc. Adjusting entries are required so that pertinent amounts are all that is included in the financial statements of a particular period.

There may be expenses that occurred very late in the accounting period, and these could not be processed or recorded in the general ledger accounts. To include these expenses in the financial statements, accrual type adjusting entries will have to be recorded by the accountant.

GAAP also required other adjusting entries like adjustments for uncollectible accounts receivable or adjustments for some marketable securities if the fair market value is different.

Accounting periods

Corporations are compelled to issue their annual financial statements. However, it is also common for them to prepare these financial statements every month. The period can be anything from a month, three months, six months, a year, etc. A lot of companies have their accounting year beginning on 1st January and end on 31st December. However, others could have a financial year that begins on 1st July in one year and ending on 30th June of next year. Such financial years are called fiscal years. Certain companies have fiscal years based on weeks and not months as well. A fiscal year is beneficial because it will coincide with a business year.

Users of financial statements

Financial statements that are issued by a company will find their way to the following people or groups:

- Current lenders
- Current stockholders
- Potential future lenders
- Potential future investors
- Financial analysts
- Current as well as future goods and services suppliers
- Certain customers
- Labor unions
- Government agencies
- Competitors

Users tend to compare financial statements to previous accounting periods or other companies. This is why it is important that the common reporting rules are followed in the financial statements. You have learned about the requirements of GAAP in a previous section of the book.

Capital and Revenue Expenditure and Receipts

Final accounts are prepared at the end of the year and they consist of the income statement, balance sheet, cash flow statement, and the statement of retained earnings. All the accounts, which appear in the trial balance, are taken to either the income statement or the balance sheet. In order to decide which item goes where, the following principle of accounting is applied. All revenue expenditures along with receipts are taken to the income statement while all capital expenditure and capital receipts are entered in the balance sheet. It is, therefore, essential to realize the importance of distinction between capital and revenue items because any error in these items can lead to falsification of final accounts.

A capital expenditure is one that increases the value at which a fixed or a capital asset may properly be carried on in the books. All expenditure that results in the acquisition of any permanent assets that are intended to be continually used in the business purpose of earning revenue I'd deem to be capital expenditure. The term capital expenditure is usually used for signifying an expenditure, which increases the quantity of fixed assets, quality of fixed assets, or results in the replacement of fixed assets.

An amount that is spent by the business for earning or providing revenue is referred to as revenue expenditure. Revenue expenditure is one that constitutes a proper deduction from income revenue. It is an expense. In other words, all establishments and other expenses incurred in the conduct and administration of the business are deemed to be revenue expenditures. All expenses incurred by the way of repairs, replacement of existing assets, which not only add to their earning capacity but simply serve to maintain the original equipment in an efficient working condition are charged as revenue expenditures. Examples of revenue expenses include any expenditure incurred during the normal course of business. For instance, expenses of Administration, expenses incurred in manufacturing and selling products, expenses related to salaries, rent and repair of facets and so on. All those expenses which are incurred for maintaining the business like the replacement of any existing permanent assets, costs of stores consumed for manufacturing and so on are also deemed to be revenue expenditures.

Deferred revenue expenditure is the term that's used for describing any expenditure of a revenue nature with its benefits spread over a couple of years. Some common examples of deferred revenue income include preliminary expenses, brokerage payable on issue of shares, expenses incurred in shifting a business, or even any exceptional repairs. All these might look like expenses but when it comes to accounting, they aren't treated as regular expenses. Given the massive amounts involved, these expenses cannot be written off in a single financial year. If such expenses are written off from a single year's profits, then there might be no profits left. To prevent this and to maintain a profitable venture, deferred revenue expenses are written off from the income statement on a yearly basis. The unwritten portion of the deferred revenue expenditure will be reflected on the assets side of the balance sheet.

All capital receipts are reflected in the balance sheet and the revenue receipts in the income statements. Capital receipts include the proceeds from the sale of fixed assets, issue of any shares or debentures, and money received in the form of loans. Any funds obtained in the due course of business are known as revenue receipts. Revenue receipts include any proceeds from the sale of goods, interest received on deposits, or even dividend on any investments.

Income Statement

Income statements are financial statements that report the revenues, expenses, and net income of a company. The balance sheet of a company is concerned only with a particular point in time. However, the income statement will cover a period of a time interval.

Amongst other financial statements, the income statement is an important statement that accountants or business owners use. It is also referred to as a statement of income, statement of operators or profit and loss statement.

It is important because it will indicate the profitability of that company in a specific time interval that is mentioned in its heading. This period of time will be decided by the business and can vary for everyone. Remember that the income statement will show expenses, losses, gains, and revenues. It will not show cash disbursements or cash receipts.

The profitability of the company is given special attention due to various reasons. For instance, when a company cannot operate profitably, a bank or creditor will be unwilling to provide any more funds to the company. However, if the company is working profitably, it will be demonstrating its ability to use any borrowed money successfully. Lenders or investors need to see if the company has the ability to function profitably before they know they can invest more money in it. It is also of concern to others like competitors, labor unions, consonant management or government agencies.

Items included

The income statement format will vary depending on the complexity of the business activities of a company. However, the following elements will be included in the income statements for most companies:

Revenues and gains

Operating revenue

All the income that comes from primary activities of a business is referred to as operating revenue. For instance, if a company is involved in the manufacturing of a product, then the revenue from primary activities will be the income obtained from the sale of its products. For a wholesaler, the operating revenue will come from the sales of the products he offers. Likewise, for a company that offers services, the operating revenue will be generated from the fees or revenue earned in exchange for its services.

Net-operating revenue

Any income generated from the non-core or secondary activities of a business is known as non-operating income. This income originates from earnings that are generated from sources other than the sale and purchase of goods or services. It usually includes any income that business earns from its investments, rental income from business property, receipts of royalty payment, or any other income generated from advertising placed on the business's property.

Gains

Gains are also referred to as other income. This refers to the net income, which was made from other activities such as the sale of any long-term assets. It also includes any income that was realized from a one-time activity, which isn't related to the business like the sale of a subsidiary company, of unused land, or any other property owned by the business. Revenue and receipts are two different things. Any income, which is made from the sales of products or services provided will be termed as revenue for a specific period. Receipts refer to the cash that is received and will be accounted for only when the money is actually received. For instance, if a customer purchases goods on credit on 15th September and promises to repay by 15th October, then this transaction will be recorded only when the amount is actually received by the business.

Expenses and losses

The cost that business in cause to continue its operations and earn a profit is referred to as an expense. There are certain expenses that can be written off as a tax return if the IRS guidelines provide for it.

Primary activity expenses

All the expenses that a business incurs in its usual day-to-day operations, which are directly associated with the primary activity of the business are referred to as primary activity expenses. Primary activity expenses include selling costs, administrative expenses, depreciation, R&D expenses, cost of goods sold, and even amortization. The usual items included in this section include the wages payable to workers, salaries payable to employees, expenses toward utility bills, and sales commissions.

Secondary activity expenses

All the expenses incurred by a business that are directly related to its primary activities are referred to as secondary activity expenses. It usually includes expenses like any interest paid on loan. Losses are also treated as expenses. Any loss that is incurred from the sale of a long-term asset or any other unusual costs such as unexpected lawsuits will be treated as expenses.

The primary expenses and revenue of business provide insight into whether the company's core business is doing well or not. Whereas, the secondary expenses and revenue accounts show the company's expertise while managing its non-core activities. If the income from the sale of the goods produced by a company is lower than the income that it receives from interest on the bank account, it shows that accompanies and utilizing its funds properly. If the company is gaining any recurring income by hosting billboards at a factory, then it shows that the company is capitalizing on its resources and increasing its profitability. The income statement essentially shows whether the company's funds are being utilized optimally or not.

The formula used for calculating the Net Income is as follows.

Net Income = (Gains + Revenue) – (Expenses + Losses)

ACCOUNTING

Let us look at an example to get a better understanding of the way that income is calculated. Let us assume that a fictitious company, ABC produces sports merchandise and offers sports training too. The company received a total of $25,000 from the sale of its goods in the first quarter. It also received an additional $5000 from the training services it offers. Its primary expenses amounted to $10,500. It also received $1000 from the sale of unused machinery and lost $800 from the settlement of a lawsuit. So, the net income of this company comes to $19700.

This is referred to as a single-step income statement. It is perhaps the simplest forms of income statement there is. However, seldom do companies in the real world have such straightforward income statements. Most companies have a rather diversified array of business segments and usually, get involved in mergers or acquisitions and also form any strategic partnerships. Given the complexities of a modern-day company, they usually follow a multi-step income statement. In this method, all the different items listed in an income statement are segregated.

The net amount should be positive when the expenses and losses are subtracted from revenues and gains. This will be labeled as net income. It will be a net loss if the net amount comes out to be negative.

Amounts on Income statements

The amounts that are shown on the company's income statement will reflect many transactions that the accounting system recorded. Adjusting entry amounts will also be entered to comply with the accrual accounting method.

Revenues are what the company earns from its main activities. This will include selling products that are reported as net product revenue, net sales, etc. It will also include providing services that are reported as revenues or net service revenues. Revenues will be reported in the income statement in that period in which they are earned. These are captured when the sales invoices are usually prepared. Accountants prepare adjusting entries at the end of that accounting period and include any revenue that might not have been processed by the accounting system as well.

Expenses are historical costs associated with the main business activities of a company and reported on their income statement. Costs end up as expenses in income statements in four ways. One is when they beat match revenues. The second is when they were used or expired. The third is when no future value is there that can be measured. The fourth is when the cost is too small for justifying allocation to a future period.

Gains and losses are recorded on disposals of assets. The received amount should not be included in revenues when an asset is it longer used by a company.

Balance Sheet

Balance sheets are statements of financial position. They reflect the accounting equation of a company or sole proprietor. These balance sheets will report the assets, liabilities, and stockholder's equity of a company at a specific point. The balance sheet is the accounting equation and will display that the company has total assets equal to the sum of its liabilities and stockholder's equity.

Accounting balance sheets are major financial statements that accountants or business owners use. Since the balance sheet will be representing the financial position of the company at a specific date, it is often considered a financial snapshot in time. The balance sheet will inform any reader of the financial position of the company at some point in time. This allows people like creditors to check what the company's assets and liabilities are at that point. This kind of information is valuable for bankers who need to determine whether they should approve loans or credit for a company. Current investors, suppliers, company management, labor unions, etc. are also invested in this information from the balance sheet.

The balance sheet is prepared with the primary aim to understand the desires financial position of a business on the last date of its financial year. Different balances of nominal accounts like salaries, wages, rent and commission, and so on from the trial balance transferred to the trading on the profit and loss account. Various real accounts, as well as personal accounts related to the customers, are placed under the heading- sundry debtors. Similarly, all balances due to the suppliers are grouped under the heading- sundry creditors. All real and personal account balances are grouped into two categories of assets and liabilities.

The balance sheet is a precise statement of financial position. It will be prepared only after the completion of the trading on the profit and loss account. All the items that were not included in the trading in the profit and loss account will be divided into assets and liabilities, which will find a place in the balance sheet. Liabilities to present the credit balances on the ledger, whereas the assets represent the debit balances. The balance sheet is always prepared at a specific date and shows the business's financial position on that date.

There are three important terms that are used in the balance sheet, and they are assets, equity, and liabilities. In this section, let us look at a couple of important terms that are used in the balance sheet.

As mentioned in the previous chapters, assets represent any tangible objects along with the intangible value that a business owns. Assets can be classified as fixed assets and current assets. A current asset is a term which is used to describe cash in other assets along with resources commonly believed as those which can be readily sold or consumed during the normal operating cycle of a business. The normal operating cycle of businesses about 12 months, but at times it can be longer than that. So, different prepayment of expenses like prepaid insurance, salary paid in advance, or even rent paid in advance will be classified as current assets. Other current assets include cash balance, bank balance, temporary investment, debtors, stock in trade, any payments made in advance, and all bills receivables. Any asset that provides any service or helps to increase the value of a business and is held for a longer period is defined as fixed assets. Fixed assets include tangible assets like land, equipment, plant and building, furniture and fixtures, machinery and such. It also includes intangible assets such as patents, trademarks, and goodwill.

Equity represents anything that has been enforced against the assets of a business. Claims can be made against the assets of a business by owners as well as creditors, and they are both termed as equities. So, equity refers to a claim that the following have:

- Creditors of a business,
- Owners of a business,
- Creditors as well as owners of a business.

So, Equity = Assets

Or, Liabilities + Shareholder's Equities = Assets.

Any claim that has been made against the assets of a business by the creditors is referred to as liabilities. Liabilities can include long-term liabilities of fixed liabilities and current liabilities. Please refer to the information given in "Chapter 1" to learn more about liabilities.

Cash Flow Statement

Cash flow statements are officially known as the statement of cash flows. It is one of the main financial statements of a corporation. This cash flow statement will report the cash that is generated and used in a time interval that is specified in the heading of the statement. The company can decide what this period is.

The statement of cash flow will organize and report what cash was generated or used under the following categories:

- Operating activities. Items reported on an income statement from the accrual method of accounting are converted to cash.
- Investing activities. The purchase or sale of any long-term investments, properties, plants, and equipment are reported.

- Financing activities. Insurance or repurchase of the company's bonds, stock, and dividend payments are recorded.

- Supplemental information. Exchange of any significant items not involving cash is reported. The interest and income tax amount paid is also reported.

So, what does the statement of cash flow tell you?

Income statements are prepared with the help of accrual basis of accounting. Due to this, there is a change that the revenues were not collected. The expenses that were reported on that income statement might also not have been paid. The balance sheet changes can be reviewed to determine what the facts are. However, the cash flow statement will have integrated this information already. This is why cash flow statements are utilized by savvy businesspeople or investors.

Points to note are:

- Other than cash, if an asset increases, there will be a decrease in the cash account.

- Other than cash, if an asset decreases, there will be an increase in the cash account.

- There will be an increase in cash account if liability increases.
- There will be a decrease in the cash account if liability decreases.
- There will be an increase in cash account if there is an increase in owner's equity.
- There will be a decrease in cash account if there is a decrease in owner's equity.

Cash flow statement format

There are four distinct sections in a cash flow statement:

- Cash involving operating activities
- Cash involving investing activities
- Cash involving financing activities
- Supplemental information

If the indirect method is used to prepare the statement of cash flow, important information can be acquired from the differences in the balance sheet accounts of a company.

Cash involving operating activities:

This section will report the net income of the company and also convert it to cash basis from the accrual basis with the changes in the balances of current liability and current asset accounts like:

- Accounts receivable
- Supplies
- Inventory
- Prepaid insurance
- Notes payable
- Accounts payable
- Wages payable
- Payroll taxes payable
- Unearned revenues
- Interest payable
- Other current assets
- Other current liabilities

This section will also have adjustments for depreciation expenses, losses, and gains from long-term asset sales.

Cash involving investing activities

This section will report the changes in the long-term asset account balances like:

- Land
- Equipment
- Long term investment
- Vehicles
- Furniture

It involves the sale or purchase of any long-term investment, plant, property, and equipment.

Cash involving financing activities

This section will report the balance changes of longer-term liabilities and stockholder's equity accounts like:

- Bonds payable
- Preferred stock
- Notes payable
- Common stock
- Deferred income taxes
- Treasury stock

Retained earnings

These financial activities will involve repurchase or issuance of the company's bonds or stocks and also borrowings or repayments that are long term and short term.

Supplemental information

This section in the statement will disclose the interest amount and paid income taxes. Significant exchanges that did not involve cash will also be reported.

Certain adjustments are made to the net income of a company by adding or subtracting any differences in revenue, credit transactions, and expenses. These adjustments help calculate the cash flow of a business. All non-cash items are included in the income statement, whereas all assets and liabilities are included in the balance sheet. The cash flow statement helps fill up the gap between these two statements by making a place for all the adjustments made by a business. There are two methods that can be used for preparing the cash flow statement, and they are the direct method and the indirect method.

Direct method

The direct method is quite straightforward. It essentially is a summation of the different types of cash payments as well as the receipts of a company. It includes the cash paid to suppliers, cash received from customers, and any cash paid out as salaries. All these figures are calculated by using the opening and closing balances of different types of business accounts. It helps to examine any net increase or decrease in business accounts.

Indirect method

The cash flow from operating activities in the indirect method is calculated by using the net income of a company from its income statement. Since the income statement of a company is prepared on the accrual basis, revenue will only be recognized when it is turned and not when received. The net income is not an accurate representation of the cash flow from operating activities. There are certain items that affect the net income, and it becomes quintessential to adjust any earnings before interest and taxes. This needs to be done even if no cash has been paid or received against them. The indirect method also makes provisions for adding back any non-operating activities that don't affect the operating cash flow of a company. For instance, depreciation is not a cash expense. Depreciation is the amount that is deducted from the value of an asset. Since it is not a cash expense, it must be added to the net sales to calculate the cash flow for the company. Only when an asset is sold will the income from might be included in a cash flow statement.

Accounts receivable

There will be certain changes in the accounts receivable present on a balance sheet from an accounting period to the other. This change needs to be represented in the cash flow statement. If the amount of accounts receivable decreases, it shows that more cash has entered the organization. This is usually in the form of cash received because customers are paying off their credit accounts. The amount by which the accounts receivable has decreased will be added to the net sales. If the accounts receivable has increased from one period to the next, then the increase needs to be deducted from the net sales.

Inventory value

If a company purchases raw material and spends more of its funds doing this, then there will be an increase in the inventory. If the inventory was acquired using cash, then any increase in the value of the inventory will be deducted from the net sales of the company. Likewise, any decrease in the inventory will be added to the net sales. There will be an increase in accounts payable if the inventory was purchased on credit, and the same will be reflected on the balance sheet. The amount of increase from one year to the other in inventory levels will be added to the net sales. The same criteria are used for taxes payable, prepaid insurance, and any salaries payable. If an expense has been paid off, then the difference between the value owed from one year and the next must be subtracted from the net income. If there is an outstanding amount, then any differences need to be added to the net earnings.

Investing activities

Any sources of cash, along with its use from a company's investments, are referred to as investing activities. For instance, purchase or sale of an asset, payments received from customers or loans made to a vendor, or any payments related to a merger and acquisition will be included in this category. Essentially, investing activities relates to any changes in assets, investments, or equipment related to cash generated from investing. Any changes from investing activities are referred to as cash out items since cash needs to be spent on acquiring new equipment or other short-term assets. However, whenever a company sells or divests its assets, the transaction is a cash-in since cash is entering the business.

Financing activities

The cash that is used for and incurred from financing activities is included in the section. It includes the source of cash from investors or banks and also the cash, which was used for paying any shareholders. So, the payment of dividends, payment made to repurchase talk, and along with the repayment of debt will be included in this category. Whenever capitalists raised, there will be cash from financing activities. Likewise, when a dividend is paid, it is a cash-out transaction. So, if a company issues its shares to the public, the company will receive financing. However, whenever it pays dividends to its shareholders, the company's cash reserves will reduce.

Positive cash flow is always a sign of a healthy business. It isn't necessary that a cash flow statement needs always to represent a positive cash flow. It doesn't mean that negative cash flow is a red flag. At times, negative cash flow can be because a company is expanding its business. By analyzing any changes in the cash flow from one period to the next will enable an investor to understand whether a company is performing well or not.

Balance sheet and income statement

A cash flow statement is prepared using the information collected from the income statement and the balance sheet. The net earnings calculated from the income statement is the balance from which all the other information included in the cash flow statement is deducted. Any net cash flow in the cash flow statement from one year to the next needs to be equal to the increase or decrease of cash reserves between the two consecutive balance sheets is applicable to the period within which the cash flow statement is created. For instance, if the cash flow is calculated for the year 2018, then the balance sheet from the year 2017 and 2018 need to be used.

A cash flow statement is a valuable tool, which helps to measure the profitability and the strength of a company. It helps determine whether a company has sufficient funds for meeting its expenses or not. It also helps to predict the future cash flow of the business. It is often used while budgeting. The cash flow statement provides investors with a bird's eye view of the company's financial health. The greater the cash available, the better is it for the company. It also helps the investor understand whether the company is optimally using its funds or not.

Statement of Retained Earnings

Retained earnings are the cumulative amount of earnings from the time a corporation was formed minus the amount of the cumulative dividend that it has declared since then. Simply put, retained earnings are the past earnings of the corporation that have not been distributed to stockholders of the corporation. The retained earnings of a corporation are reported separately in stockholders' equity section of a balance sheet. Even when there is a significantly large amount of positive retained earnings in a corporation, it cannot be assumed that they subsequently have a lot of cash. Corporations tend to use their cash to buy a new property, plant, or equipment. They might also use it to reduce the liabilities of the company. When the retained earnings of the corporation are a negative amount, the term "deficit" will be used and not retained earnings.

Statement of retained earnings is a statement that will show the changes from one point to another in retained earnings.

The retained earnings of a corporation are not distributed to their stockholders as dividends because the money is used for strengthening the financial position of the company. It is also used of expansion of operations or for keeping up with inflation even while trying to maintain the current operations. The corporation requires the money for various purposes.

Stockholders may ask to prefer to have the money used for such purposes because it will help increase the value of the company's stock. This is why they prefer foregoing dividends and instead want better use made of retained earnings. For individuals who are in the higher income tax brackets, getting dividends would mean that 40% of their money goes towards taxes. However, if they forego the dividend, their stock value will increase, and no tax payments are involved. When they sell their stock, they will just have to pay a much lower tax towards capital gains.

The equation used for computing the retained earnings of a company is as follows.

Retained earnings at the end = Retained earnings at the beginning + Net income – Dividends.

Chapter Six: Managerial Accounting

Managerial accounting is also known as management accounting or cost accounting. It is the process that involves identification, measurement, analysis, interpretation as well as communication of information to managers to attain the goals of their company. The main difference network financial accounting and managerial accounting is that the latter is aimed at helping managers within the organization to make decisions while the former is aimed at helping people outside the organization.

Managerial accounting will include any part of accounting that is aimed at providing business operations metrics to management. The information that is related to product cost or services is used by managerial accountants. Budgets are also used for the plan of operation of a business in a quantitative way of expression. Managerial accountants will utilize all performance reports to check for any deviation in the actual results from the given budget.

Marginal Analysis

Determination of the incremental change in profit or other gain associated with many possible alternatives is done using Marginal Analysis. The decision of choosing the alternative depends on the outcome of the analysis. A wise man must always choose the alternative that provides the maximum incremental profit. The above concept is used to maximize an organization's gains. The marginal analysis concepts are followed in many aspects, and some of them are:

- Manufacturer decision: if additional units should be sold at a reduced price to a customer.
- Personal decision: if you should do overtime or take a vacation
- Government decision: if the government should fund a public program to offer better or extra services to taxpayers.

For instance, an ice-cream parlor owner gets an order from a customer for 100 choc-bars at a price of $20 each. The ice-cream parlor owner calculates and estimates a good profit on 80 units. After that the remaining 20 units, he will have to pay his staff overtime, which doesn't make any profit from the remaining 20 units. So marginal analysis concept tells him to take an order of 80 units and make extra 20 units only if the customer pays extra money for the remaining 20 units.

Another example – suppose a phone manufacturing company is working very hard and producing the maximum number of phones up to their capacity. Still, there is more demand for these phones on the market.

So, the management will be hesitant to invest in opening an additional production center. Instead, they invest in expanding the current production facility in small increments and check if the profit margin is still maintained, so this is a marginal analysis where the management is careful and taking better decisions in expanding than to build another reproduction facility and not know if the profit can be achieved accordingly.

Contribution margin analysis

Contribution margin analysis produces the residual margin after variable expenditures are subtracted from the total revenue. The amount of money spent on various products and services can be differentiated using contribution margin analysis, from which the management can then decide which products are doing better and which of them should be focused more by increasing the ad campaign and better marketing plans. Management can compare the contribution made and the total amount of fixed costs to be given in each period of time so that the management comes to an end if the current pricing and the cost value of the business is going to make profits or not

Contribution margin is calculated by subtraction all variable expenses from the revenue. The percentage contribution margin is generated by dividing the outcome with the revenue. Overhead cost is not mentioned in this calculation.

Contribution margin analysis is also used to determine the contributions of achievement targets under the process, to check if anyone would pay enough cash for a product or a service. And if it's not worth, the in-charge must then decide if the price should be reduced so that therein profit and sale increases also.

The disadvantage of this type of analysis is that it doesn't consider the impact of products and services on the company's constraint; it's the main component for a company's high-profit achievement. When a high contribution margin product takes a longer time than the usual time, the end result would be less profit all in all because the other products are made in the remaining time and very limited time is left at the constraint. The above-mentioned conflict can be resolved by increasing the contribution margin analysis to envelope the consumption of the contribution per minute in the given time. Companies should focus on the products and services with the highest margin per minute, as they should be selling faster.

Some of the aspects are not given proper attention, and one of them is the price points included in the calculation of the contribution margin analysis. It can, in fact, be of great significance based on its use of volume discounts, special promotions, which will eventually lead to high revenue portion, which can lead to high expected contribution margins.

Constraint Analysis

Constraint analysis concentrates on the bottlenecks in an organization. So, the manager of a company should be concentrating only on the maximum usage of a bottleneck as the bottleneck helps to increase the profits of the business. Other than the bottleneck, other aspects will bring no change in profit. It's a very important concept as bottleneck can be found in any part of the business. For example, if a production company requires a high degree of technical knowledge and all the staff members of the company are fully occupied, then the sales or profit is not going to increase unless the company hires new staff members. And another example is if a production company produces 100 units of candies unless they don't buy a new machine, the current one cannot produce more than 100 as it produces to its maximum capacity.

The theory of constraints

The theory of constraints states any organization, or any system has a choke point, and the choke point prevents it from achieving its goals. The choke point, which is also called as bottleneck or constraint, must be managed carefully for the smooth operation of the business at any given time. Or else, it will be difficult to achieve the goals. The cause of the above-mentioned line is because unless the capacity of the contract is not increased, there will be no extra throughput (subtract all variable expenses from revenue).

The theory of constraints goes against the usual orthodox method of doing business, in which all the operations are performed at their maximum capacity level. From constraints point of view, maximizing all the performances of the business means it will increase the inventory, which will pile up, without any increase in profit. Therefore, proving that increasing the operations will only lead to an increase in inventory and not in profit.

Example of a constrained operation

A sofa production company finds out that their bottleneck is sponge production. Sponge production can produce only 30 sponges in a day and not more than that. So, if the company makes more than 30 sofa parts, then the remaining parts after 25 units should be kept in the storeroom. And it will only keep peeling and increase the cost of working capital.

So, the manager then finds out that it is wisest to return to only 30 units - production of all parts along with the sponge - so that the production and profit consistency remains stable.

Inventory buffers

It is extremely important to maximize the capacity in a constrained operation every time. One of the best ways to do it is by building an inventory buffer in front of the constraint operation. This inventory buffer will assure that any shortage of production of any parts of the operation will not hamper the continuous process or production of the product and it usually fluctuates in size as it gets used and replenished.

The performance of a company can improve by installing a sprint capacity in the production areas of the company.

Sprint Capacity

Sprint capacity is an increasingly high amount of production capacity that is assembled in the factories or workstations. When a mishap happens in the factory, and it cannot be avoided, the continuous flow of parts is stopped, and that's when sprint capacity is required. In this phase, the bottleneck takes resources from inventory buffer, which ends up in shortage in inventory buffer. So extra sprint capacity is required to mass-produce parts to refill the parts shortage in inventory buffer so that it can be used in the next unavoidable mishap.

It's a wise decision to invest in a large sprint capacity in a production company as it can rebuild the inventory buffer is a short span of time. So, if you can invest in a large sprint capacity, only a small investment is required for investment buffer. Or else if you invest in large inventory buffer, there will be less sprint capacity.

ACCOUNTING

One of the main points we can learn here is that it is always a better option to maintain some space in the capacity in work areas and not limit the production capacity to the current needs.

Capital Budgeting

It is almost every company's motive and aims to expand their company in the future, and it is only possible if the company has good capital or good assets. And this capital, budgeting plays an important part in this process.

Every company uses a formal procedure to evaluate any potential investments or expenditures of significant value. This process is known as capital budgeting. It usually involves different decisions related to investing any existing funds for addition, modification, replacement, or even disposition of any fixed assets. Every company keeps making large expenditures from time to time. A couple of instances of large expenditures include the purchase of any fixed assets, acquiring new equipment, research and development projects, and so on. Each of these types of projects requires a rather large sum to be spent, and they are known as capital expenditures. Capital budgeting enables a company to maximize its future profits because a company can manage only a small number of massive projects at any given time.

Capital budgeting usually involves the following.

- The calculation of any future profit which can be generated by a project within a given period,
- The cash flow for a future period,
- The present value of the cash flow, along with the time value of money,
- The time is taken by the project to realize the initial investment,
- Risk analysis of the project and other factors.

Capital refers to the total investment made in a company, and budgeting is all about creating budgets and plans.

Some of the examples of capital expenditures are:

- Buying new equipment
- Repairing old equipment
- Buying delivery vehicles
- Constructing additions to old buildings

Few examples of Capital Budgeting Calculations

Capital budgeting includes the following calculations for every single project:

- Future accounting profit by period
- Future cash flows by period
- The present value of the cash flows by reducing them with an appropriate interest rate

- The time period is taken for a project's cash flow to return the initial cash investment
- An assessment of risk with the need to complete a project

Forecasting in Accounting

The process of utilizing the current and older cost data to predict future cost is called forecasting in accounting. It is important for organization purposes - it is important for a company to do estimation and organize money incurred before the actually incurring begins. These are the following methods used to forecast cost accounting:

- High-low method cost estimation
- Budgeting
- Regression analysis

Budgeting

Budgeting is the process of preparing a budget in order to plan for revenues and expenditures in an upcoming fiscal duration.

There are four objectives of budgeting, and these are the following:

- Facilitate the coordination and communication of these plans across the organization.

- Allocation of the resources within an organization.
- Managing the financial and operational performance of the members during the fiscal period.
- Evaluation of performances and producing goal-based incentives.

Budgets are made using current and historical data and estimations about upcoming trends. Traditional methods or zero-based methods can be used to prepare budgets. In the traditional method, they track the previous period's budgets and use it at the beginning of the upcoming period's budget whereas in the zero-based budget method they don't use any older records and start from scratch in each period.

High-low method

A method of estimating the forecasting is called high low method. It's a very simple method of estimating forecasting, but the accuracy is less than the more sophisticated methods like regression analysis.

In this technique, a set of data is required, which relates the cost-to-cost driver activities.

So, you have to consider the maximum cost and maximum cost driver activity and the minimum cost and minimum cost driver activity from the data set. Then you have to take out these four parts of the data to calculate the slope of the line, which connects two points. At last, you figure out the intercept using the slope and one of the points. And the end result will be the high, low-cost equation for that exact cost incurring activity.

Regression Analysis

A method of relating a dependent variable to an independent variable is known as regression analysis. This technique mainly functions to find out the value of the variance in the dependent variable due to variations in the independent variable. A set of data from both the dependent variable and the independent variable is required in regression analysis. The best platform for this analysis is in a computer program.

Regression analysis is of two types, and that is simple and multiple. In simple regression analysis, only one dependent variable and the independent variable is used. In multiple regression analysis, several independent variables are used, and only one dependent variable. The final outcome is it is an equation, which is used to predict costs depending on specific estimates of independent adjustable activity.

Cost Accounting

As the name suggests, cost accounting is that branch accounting which deals with companies cost of production. It does this by considering the input cost of every step of production along with fixed costs like depreciation of any fixed capital or capital equipment. All these costs are first individually recorded and measured. Once this is done, then the input results are compared with the output of all the actual results. Cost accounting enables management to measure the financial performance of a company. Cost accounting is used for decision-making. Financial accounting is the data, which is available to the investors. Financial accounting is the representation of different costs and financial performance, which includes the liabilities as well as the assets of a company. Cost accounting is one of the most beneficial tools for management while setting up any cost control programs and budgets to improve the net margins of the organization in the future. The main difference between financial accounting and cost accounting is that in financial accounting the costs are classified based on the type of transactions, whereas in cost accounting, the costs are classified based on the information required by the management. Unlike financial accounting, cost accounting doesn't have to follow any predefined rules or principles. Since it is a tool for internal management, it doesn't have to abide by the GAAP.

A lot of people tend to believe that cost accounting came about during the time of the industrial revolution. The growing economy of the industrial forces of demand and supply forced manufacturers to track the levels of there's talk along with the price of the same.

Somewhere around the early 19th century, when David Ricardo was developing economic theories, famous writers like Charles Babbage were writing guides about how a business can manage its internal cost accounting. Cost accounting became an integral part of business management by the beginning of the 20th century.

Types of cost accounting

There are various types of cost accounting, and they are as follows.

Standard cost accounting

This form of cost accounting is based on ratios that are used to compare optimal use of labor along with material for producing goods or services under given conditions. Accessing and analyzing these differences is known as variance analysis. Traditionally, cost accounting essentially allocates costs based on a unit measure like labor or machine hours. Since the beginning of standard cost accounting, there has been a proportional increase in overhead costs and labor costs. Therefore, if the overhead cost is allocated as the overall cost, it doesn't always produce accurate insights. One of the major problems associated cost accounting is that this kind of accounting places more emphasis on labor efficiency than anything else. These days, labor efficiency makes for only a relatively small cost for most of the modern companies.

Activity-based costing

According to this form of cost, the overheads from every department are taken, and they are assigned to specific cost objects like customers, products, or services. An activity analysis is first performed to determine the way in which these costs must be assigned to their associated cost objects. During an activity analysis, the appropriate output measure is the essential cost driver. Activity-based costing is more accurate than standard cost accounting. Activity-based costing enables the management to understand the cost along with the profitability of the specific services or products offered by a company. Usually, this is conducted by passing out a survey to the employees of an organization who will then account for the time that they spend on different tasks. This gives the management a clear idea about the tasks that are time-consuming and the past in which most of the funds are spent.

Marginal costing

It is believed to be a simpler version of cost accounting. In marginal costing, the relationship that exists between the sales price of a product or service and the quantum of sales, the number of products produced, expenses incurred, costs, and the profits. This relationship is referred to as contribution margin. The contribution margin is usually obtained by dividing the revenue after subtracting any variable costs by the total revenue. This analysis is often used to understand the impact of changing cost on any potential profits. All the different factors that can influence the potential profit earning ability of the company can be analyzed by using marginal costing.

Types of costs

There are different types of costs, and they are fixed costs, variable costs, direct costs, and operating costs. Any cost that doesn't change according to the amount of work accompanied as is referred to as a fixed cost. The fixed cost usually includes items like the payment of rent on a building or a piece of equipment that they appreciate at a fixed value every month. Also, costs that change according to the company's level of production are referred to as variable cost.

The amount spent on making a product is known as product cost. The product cost includes direct materials, direct labor, consumable production supplies, and factory overhead. It can also be said that product cost is the cost of the labor needed to perform a service to a customer. In advanced cases, product cost also includes the total cost of a service provided like compensation, payroll taxes, and employee benefits. All those costs that are related to the day-to-day operations of the business are known as operating costs. These costs can be either a variable or fixed according to the given situation.

All the costs that are directly related to the production of a product are direct costs. For instance, if a coffee roaster spends about six hours roasting coffee beans, then the direct costs will include the cost of the coffee beans along with the cost of the labor.

Product cost

The product cost on a unit basis is derived by adding the total amount spent on direct labor, direct materials, consumable supplies, allocated overhead and the sum are divided by the total number of units.

The formula for calculating the product cost is as follows:

(Total direct labor + Total direct materials + Consumable supplies + Total allocated overhead) ÷ Total number of units = Product unit cost

This cost can be considered as an inventory asset of a company if the product is not sold. As soon as the product sells, the amount can be charged on the cost of the products sold. Then it will be mentioned as an expense on the revenue statement.

Product cost is mentioned in the financial statement of a company as it includes the production overhead that is required by GAAP and IFRS both. Managers can alter the product cost to cut the overhead component when they make short-term production and sale price decision. Some of the managers can also choose to concentrate more on the effect of a product on a bottleneck operation, which clearly indicates that they are focusing mainly on the total direct material cost of a product and the total time spent on bottleneck operation.

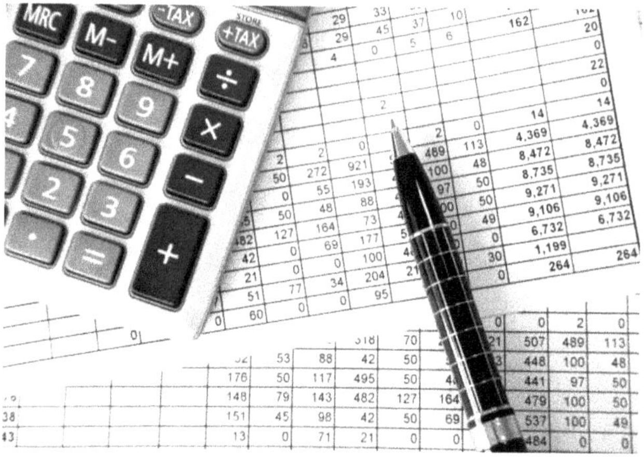
MRC
-TAX
STORE
+TAX
M-
M+

Conclusion

As we come to the end of the book, I would like to thank you again. I hope the book was helpful and you now have a much better understanding of accounting than you did before. You can see that a lot more is involved in accounting than the layman usually thinks. However, it is not really as complicated as some may think either. Understanding the basic concepts play a large role in it. Using the information given in this book, you can soon be on your way to becoming a great accountant. All the information in this book has been gathered from renowned and trustworthy sources. I hope it has helped you gain enough knowledge on financial and managerial accounting. Most of your questions on this subject will be answered if you read through the book thoroughly. Nonetheless, there is a lot of material available on accounting and you can always learn more.

If you found this book helpful, you may even recommend it to anyone else who needs a little help on the subject of accounting.

Thank you again and I wish you luck!

www.ingramcontent.com/pod-product-compliance
Lightning Source LLC
Chambersburg PA
CBHW071424210326
41597CB00020B/3647